the soul's slow ripening

"Christine Valters Painter has written another excellent book for spiritual seekers desiring insight, encouragement, and inspiration on their spiritual paths. In *The Soul's Slow Ripening*, she provides readers a series of practices inspired by the Irish traditions that will help readers, as she says, live into 'new ways of being' by pursuing such helpful practices as working with dreams, going on pilgrimages, having a soul friend, and seeking solitude. I cannot recommend enough this practical guide to soul-making."

Edward C. Sellner
Author of *Wisdom of the Celtic Saints*

"What a delight to encounter this rich, multi-layered text in which we are given practices informed by Celtic spirituality and the lives of the Celtic saints! Meant for savoring, *The Soul's Slow Ripening* invites us to remember insights treasured by Celtic Christians and to incorporate those ways of praying into daily life."

Mary C. Earle
Author of *Celtic Christian Spirituality*

"*The Soul's Slow Ripening* is a threshold experience you didn't know your soul was longing for. But then, you crack the cover, turn the pages, and watch in wonder as Christine Valters Paintner takes you gently by the hand and invites you to walk in, and through, and around twelve heart-expanding Celtic practices. Along the way, you realize that you, too, have a wild and sacred Celtic heart."

Janet Conner
Host of *The Soul-Directed Life* and author of *Find Your Soul's Purpose*

"Celtic Spirituality is an embodied spirituality—a path of poetry, creativity, and intuition. Christine Valters Paintner guides the wisdom of the Celts straight into the heart with her wonderful mix of stories and practices. *The Soul's Slow Ripening* shows us the way to walk this ancient path today."

Carl McColman
Author of *Befriending Silence*

12 CELTIC PRACTICES
for
SEEKING THE SACRED

The soul's slow ripening

christine valters paintner

SORIN BOOKS   Notre Dame, IN

"Self-Portrait" from *Fire in the Earth* by David Whyte is printed with permission from Many Rivers Press. Copyright © 1992 Many Rivers Press, P.O. Box 868, Langley, WA 98260.

Scripture quotations are from *New Revised Standard Version Bible*, copyright © 1989 National Council of the Churches of Christ in the United States of America. Used by permission. All rights reserved.

---

www.sorinbooks.com

Paperback: ISBN-13 978-1-932057-10-2

E-book: ISBN-13 978-1-932057-11-9

Cover image © gettyimages.com.

Cover and text design by Brian C. Conley.

Printed and bound in Canada.

Library of Congress Cataloging-in-Publication Data is available.

To my much-beloved husband, John,
who joined me so wholeheartedly on this
adventure to live and work in Ireland.

contents

introduction
ix

1. The practice of Thresholds
I

2. The practice of Dreaming
13

3. The practice of *peregrinatio* and
seeking your place of Resurrection
25

4. The practice of Blessing Each Moment
39

5. The practice of soul Friendship
53

6. The practice of Encircling
69

7. The practice of walking the Rounds
81

8. The practice of Learning by Heart
93

9. The practice of solitude and silence
105

10. The practice of seasonal cycles
119

11. The practice of Landscape as Theophany
133

12. The Practice of Three Essential Things
143

Conclusion
155

Acknowledgments
157

Appendix 1: Contemplative Photography and Lectio Divina
159

Appendix 2: Resources in Celtic Christian Spirituality
163

Notes
165

introduction

In 2007, my husband, John, and I made our first trip to Ireland together. I had been once to Dublin as a child with my parents but
did not remember much of it. We set off on a three-week journey,
with him driving on the opposite side of the road than we were used
to and me trying to navigate in a country with a low commitment
to good road signs. We went from Dublin to Waterford, around to
Cashel and Kenmare, to Dingle and Galway, to Westport, and then
back to Dublin again. It was a wonderful adventure. While we were
traveling, I read Thomas Cahill's now-classic book *How the Irish
Saved Civilization*, in which he describes the essential role of the Irish
monks and their work on illuminating manuscripts during the Dark
Ages. I was captivated, especially by the idea that Ireland was outside the Roman Empire and the form of Christianity developed early
on was indigenous and localized. Because this indigenous Christianity was introduced without violence, it aligned with older traditions
and practices of the pagan culture and the Druids. This eventually
brought the Irish into conflict with the Roman Church around such
issues as the date of Easter and how to wear the tonsure. By the late
Middle Ages, Rome had brought conformity to these practices, but
there was a rich period from about the fifth until the eleventh century when Christianity flourished in a way that seemed to be more
earth-honoring and connected to the landscape. We call this period
Celtic Christianity.

The Celtic period in Ireland actually began about 500 BCE, and even earlier in Europe. The first Celtic remains are found in the tiny village of Hallstatt in Austria, near Salzburg, from the eighth to the sixth century BCE. During some salt mining in the mountain, many bronze artifacts and 1,300 burials were discovered from the Celtic peoples who had lived there. There is some dispute over the term *Celt* to describe the peoples of Ireland during this time period, in part because when they arrived, there was already a significant population living on the island.

Oliver Davies, in his book *Celtic Spirituality*, describes *Celtic* as an overworked term that is used to oversimplify the complexity of Irish history, but says that it is still a helpful term in what it includes. Ultimately he advocates for "a 'soft' use of Celtic, therefore, which is to be distinguished from a 'hard' use in that it denies neither the real variety of culture in the Celtic world nor the evident continuities with other cultural areas. But it does maintain the principle of an affinity of language, supporting some kind of affinity of culture between the Celtic-speaking areas, reinforced by extensive cultural contact based on close geographical proximity."[1]

In 2012, after several years of making ancestral pilgrimages to the homelands of our various maternal and paternal ancestors, John and I felt called to move to Europe.[2] It was the unfolding of a whole confluence of events that included reclaiming my Austrian citizenship through my father, earning me a European Union passport, as well as John being ready for a break from twelve years of teaching high school theology. We moved first to Vienna, Austria, for six months and then discerned we were being called to spend time in Ireland, where we had fallen in love with the land and culture on our trip five years before.

People often ask us how we ended up in Galway City, and it was largely an intuitive choice. We had only spent two nights here on our previous trip, and the full day was spent on a day trip out to the island of Inishmore. We knew we didn't want to be in Dublin but still wanted the convenience of a city. I loved the idea of being on the Atlantic Ocean, on the western edge of Ireland and the western fringe of Europe. The image of the wild edges called to me. We also knew it had a reputation for being a center for the arts. Both of these factors sparked our imaginations, so that was enough to draw us.

When we moved to Galway, I knew that Ireland had been a thriving community of monks for centuries, but I had no idea just how saturated the landscape was with the ruins of these ancient monasteries. Within an hour's drive of us are dozens of sites. We started visiting them, some on the recommendations of new friends, some with local guides, and some we just stumbled upon on our own. Despite the buildings being "ruins," we were entranced by these places. The roofs were gone from many of them, opening them up to the sky and the elements of creation. Irish writer John O'Donohue writes that "ruins are not empty. They are sacred places full of presence. . . . The life and passion of a person leaves an imprint on the ether of a place. Love does not remain within the heart, it flows out to build secret tabernacles in the landscape."[3] Holy wells were still places people came to seek healing. The stillness found at these locations opened us up to a beautiful sense of sacred presence where we could feel all those who had prayed in these places for hundreds of years prior.

When we first moved to Ireland, we didn't know how long our stay would last. In the first year, we decided to offer a pilgrimage to these places we were discovering, with an emphasis on a small community and slow travel. When it filled within a day, we realized there was a hunger for meaningful and contemplative travel here; this has since become a significant part of our work.

Five years into this adventure and we keep falling more and more in love with Ireland. We have bought a home in the heart of Galway City and can't imagine living anywhere else right now. We have been blessed with many friendships and the amazing hospitality of the Irish people.

The longer we live here, the more we appreciate the rich monastic tradition that weaves so beautifully with our love of both desert and Benedictine monasticism. We have also discovered the rich tradition that was already here prior to Christianity, with the Celtic and pre-Celtic periods.[4]

Oliver Davies described the way Christianity developed during the medieval period in Celtic lands, characterized by several things:

> a strongly incarnational theology, with an emphasis in diverse ways on physicality and materiality that supports both asceticism and sacramentality. Particularly in vernacular sources, nature appears as a theme to an unusual degree, and enjoys its own autonomy, rather than purely serving the human ends of atmosphere and mood. . . . Human creativity is drawn to the center of the Christian life in Irish art and Welsh poetry, both of which stress the role of the imagination. Features such as the Brigit tradition offer positive and empowering images of women, even if the relation between these and contemporary social realities is complex . . . we also find here a wonderfully life-affirming and exuberant kind of Christianity that must owe something of its spirit to pre-Christian forms of religious life among the Celts. . . . If a world religion is to take root within a community, then it is inevitable that some degree of fusion or coalescence will take place between the new religion and the religious forms it is seeking to replace.[5]

It is this fusion of the pre-Christian practices and beliefs into the particularly monastic form of Christianity that developed in Ireland that seems to attract and draw many people. There are many ways in which Ireland offers a vision for life that feels more aligned with the natural world, a way of life in which work and prayer long ago became intertwined. In his book *Celtic Christianity*, Timothy Joyce sees the attraction of the monastic experience to those already living in Ireland:

> Monasticism appealed to a warrior people who were attracted to an ascetic lifestyle. It appealed to a mystical people who had relied on Druids to interpret signs of the cosmos. It appealed to a tribal people who lived closely in community. It appealed to a marginalized people who saw the monk as one who lived on the edge of things, on the very margins of life. It appealed to a people who saw in pilgrimage and the spiritual journey the sense of adventure and quest that their ancestors had enjoyed. All these

appeals coalesced in the emergence of Christian communities based on monasticism.[6]

There has been a growing hunger over the last several years for more resources on Celtic spirituality, and there is already a rich array available. We first offered the materials in this book as part of two online retreats in our virtual community, Abbey of the Arts, to great enthusiasm. This led to the expansion of the materials into the book form that you now hold in your hands.

Go and Practice First

The Celtic monks were heavily influenced by the desert tradition before them. In the second and third centuries, men and women fled the cities and wandered out into the deserts of Egypt and Syria to find a way of life immersed in connection to the divine. They sought out *hesychia*, which is a deep inner stillness cultivated through years of contemplative practice. We are left with a collection of short sayings and stories from these desert mothers and fathers that made their way to Ireland, most likely via the sea routes that were the common way of travel at the time.

The Irish monks wanted to imitate the desert monks in seeking a place in the desert for prayer and practice. Instead of the dry and dusty landscape of the Middle East, they ventured out into the lush wilderness of Ireland and set up communities. Many of these places are called *dysert*, which means "desert place" and reflects their longing to mirror their spiritual brothers and sisters. Many of these communities were on islands dotted off the coast of the mainland. Perhaps the most striking of these is Skellig Michael, off the southwest coast of county Kerry, a small island jutting up from the Atlantic Ocean almost vertically. It is still possible to visit this place in the summer if the sea cooperates and the swells and winds are not too high. There is no dock on which to land, and the stairs that climb steeply to the top offer no handrails.

In my own spiritual life, I have largely been drawn to contemplative practices. Practices are a way of embodying the spiritual journey rather than merely thinking about it. Practices help us to bring the reality of what we seek into the physicality and earthiness of our lives. The Irish monks left behind a beautiful legacy of practices, many of which are unique to this part of the world and will be the framework for our exploration.

We start with a story from the desert fathers and mothers because this desert tradition had a significant influence on the Irish monks. It is about the practice of the spiritual life, which means an embodied way of living out our beliefs. Transformation begins with practice, a living into new ways of being.

> Abba Abraham told of a man of Scetis who was a scribe and did not eat bread. A brother came to beg him to copy a book. The old man whose spirit was engaged in contemplation, wrote, omitting some phrases and with no punctuation. The brother, taking the book and wishing to punctuate it, noticed that words were missing. So he said to the old man, "Abba, there are some phrases missing." The old man said to him, "Go, and practice first that which is written, then come back and I will write the rest."[7]

I love this story about receiving a book with missing words and punctuation. "Go, and practice first that which is written," says Abba Abraham. Do not be impatient, but deepen in the wisdom already offered here. I am reminded that I already know everything I need in this moment to live fully. There is no other book or experience that will make me more complete. Once it has been integrated through practice, I will naturally be drawn to seek more; that is the nature of a curious and hungry heart seeking intimacy with the divine. But again, the caution is to not let the words in a book become a substitute for my own deep knowing.

Practice can feel tedious at times because we want immediate results. The desert elders remind us to take the long view. Discomfort is a sign we are being stretched into new territory. We have to be willing to be uncomfortable. If we always return to what feels safe and secure, we will never give our souls the opportunity to bear fruit.

Practice can support us in surrendering all that we cling to and trust in the discomfort, the stretching apart that will set us free. I invite you into a series of practices in this book inspired by the Celtic tradition and imagination. This is not an exhaustive list, but a place to begin weaving this wisdom into our daily lives.

The Soul's Slow Ripening and Discernment

The overall theme for this book is one that has been emerging in me for several years. I love the image of ripening as an organic and slow process. Discernment calls us to tend to those moments of ripeness, as well as those times we want to pluck the fruit before it is ready, when it hasn't developed its full sweetness.

The ancient Christian monastic traditions, especially desert, Celtic, and Benedictine, offer great wisdom for this journey of unfolding. These monks understood that the soul's ripening is never to be rushed and that it takes a lifetime of work. The gift of the contemplative path is a profound honoring of the grace of slowness.

We can grow impatient when life doesn't offer us instant insights or gratification. We call on the wisdom of these monks to accompany us, to teach us what it means to honor the beauty of waiting and attending and witnessing what it is that wants to emerge, rather than what our rational minds want to make happen. The soul always offers us more richness than we can imagine, if we only make space and listen.

In 2003, I finished up a rigorous academic program, earning a PhD in Christian spirituality from the Graduate Theological Union. During the many years of my studies, the desire spurring me on was to teach at a university. But as I moved from student life into professional life as an adjunct professor at Seattle University, I found that the work wasn't as satisfying as I had hoped. I loved teaching but felt drained by the administrative duties and the limits of the curriculum. I was hungry to work with people and their lived experience.

Fifteen years prior to this, I had become immersed in Ignatian spirituality through attendance at a Jesuit college in New York and then graduate school in Berkeley, taking part in a year of the Jesuit Volunteer Corps in Sacramento, California. I participated in the Spiritual Exercises at the Mercy Center in Burlingame, California, and then as a discerning spiritual director in Seattle, Washington.

I later facilitated groups for a Jesuit extended education program in New Orleans and taught at the Jesuit Seattle University. I even worked for a couple of years at the Ignatian Spirituality Center in Seattle as their program coordinator.

There is much I love about the Jesuit order and Ignatian spirituality. Ignatius of Loyola was a genius at distilling his experiences into something that others could benefit from. Through my work and studies, I was instilled with a passion for justice and service. I met wonderful people. There are many principles from these experiences that I still draw upon in my teaching. But it wasn't until I discovered the path of monasticism that my soul felt met in a deeper way. Monasticism reflected my contemplative heart more intimately, my longing for spaciousness and silence.

I began my monastic journey through Benedictine spirituality in graduate school and then later became an oblate with a Benedictine monastery in Lacey, Washington—about an hour from Seattle, where I lived at the time. Deepening into the Rule of Benedict led me back to the desert mothers and fathers who were so influential on all of the monastic paths that followed from their example. I fell in love with the wisdom offered by their sayings and stories. Whereas Ignatius was much more systematic in his approach, the practices of the desert monks felt much more organic. This wasn't a step-by-step process for living more intimately with the divine presence but rather a gradual spiritual deepening based on stories that arose from their lives. Stories that called for savoring and living into. Stories that could break me open.

As I was beginning my university career and feeling less than satisfied, the planner in me began setting lofty goals and timelines for ways I could move into work that made me more alive: my own work of writing, spiritual direction, teaching, and leading retreats. At this time I had a powerful dream that pointed me toward a new way. In the dream, I was driving through the streets of Vienna, Austria, trying to follow a map to meet some friends who were expecting me. In through the window jumped a pair of koala bears, landing in the back seat of the car. They started distracting me and tearing the map from my hands.

Thankfully, in addition to having a contemplative heart, I also have a creative one, and dreams, symbols, and art are all important to me. As I lived into the dream, I discovered God in those koala bears, trying really hard to get the map out of my hands and asking me instead to play more. This was a moment of transformation for me, when I started to take my discernment less seriously. Around this time as well, David Whyte's poem "What to Remember When Waking" crossed my path, and the line "What you can plan is too small for you to live" shimmered brightly with truth. I started my journey toward becoming a recovering planner and letting dream wisdom inform my journey more fully, listening for synchronicities, and trusting that I didn't have to know the long-range vision of things.

In 2007, when John and I traveled to Ireland, I began to fall in love with the path of Irish monasticism. I discovered more stories and a way of moving through the world that felt more spiral and less linear, more organic and less structured. The early period of Irish monasticism is quite unique in that it was less influenced by the Roman Church and desire for uniformity of practice. The Irish monks integrated Christian teachings with the Druidic wisdom of their ancestors and created a spirituality that was much more indigenous to the place they lived.

We have found in Ireland an even richer immersion in Irish culture and ways of being in the world that are decidedly less controlled, structured, and planned than the American ways we are used to. We have learned to embrace an Irish understanding of time with more fluidity. This is challenging at times, but ultimately, it invites us into a way of being that is more relaxed and spontaneous. Even the lack of street signs invites us sometimes to get lost and disoriented and find our way anew.

Discernment is essentially a way of listening to our lives and the world around us and responding to the invitations that call us into deeper alignment with our soul's deep desires and the desires God has for us. When I work in spiritual direction, often people come at a time of discernment and transition. They have been thrust onto a threshold, often not of their own choosing, such as loss of a job or relationship. But sometimes it is born of a sense of needing a change.

Sometimes they are seeking a clear answer; they want to know the path God is calling them to, as if we each have to figure out the one right thing. My sense is that God is much more expansive than this and that God calls us to what is most life-giving, but this might take several forms, and many opportunities and possibilities. Often directees want to know their life's call, but more often than not, we can only discern what is appropriate for this particular season of our lives.

Through this journey of the last several years, I have come to embrace words such as ripening, organic, yielding, and unfolding as ways of understanding how our souls move in a holy direction. There hopefully comes a time when we have to admit that our own plans for our lives are not nearly as interesting as how our lives long to unfold—that these plans are indeed "too small" for us to live. That when we follow the threads of synchronicity, dreams, and serendipity, we are each led to a life that is rich and honoring of the soul's rhythms, which is a slow ripening rather than a fast track to discernment.

The rhythms of the seasons play a significant role in my own discernment. Honoring the flowering of spring and the fruitfulness of summer alongside the release of autumn and the stillness of winter cultivates a way of being in the world that feels deeply reverential of my body and soul's own natural cycles. We live in a culture that glorifies spring and summer energies—but autumn and winter are just as essential for rhythms of release, rest, and incubation. When we allow the soul's slow ripening, we honor that we need to come into the fullness of our own sweetness before we pluck the fruit. This takes time and patience.

The Irish tradition is deeply rooted in the landscape and the seasonal rhythms of the year. The year begins in November, as we descend into the womb of darkness. It honors wandering "for the sake of Christ," where a person may take years of journeys before settling into the "place of their resurrection." Another significant practice is walking the rounds at holy sites. Instead of a linear path straight to blessing oneself at a well, first one must walk the rounds in a "sun-wise" direction, in harmony with cosmic forces. Walking the rounds helps us to arrive, to ask permission to be there, and to slowly receive the gifts that come. Dreams show up again and again in the stories of the Irish monks as guidance for the path ahead.

The ancient Christian monastic traditions, especially desert, Celtic, and Benedictine, offer great wisdom for this journey of unfolding. They understood that the soul's ripening is never to be rushed and takes a lifetime of work.

Overview

Each chapter in *The Soul's Slow Ripening* will focus on a particular practice from the Celtic tradition that offers wisdom for the journey of discernment. We will explore the importance of thresholds, the call of dreams, the practice of *peregrinatio*, blessing, soul friendship, encircling prayer, walking the rounds, learning by heart, seeking solitude, seasonal wisdom, the landscape as theophany, and finally, three essential things.

You will also be introduced in each chapter to a story of a particular Irish saint, including such well-known names as Patrick, Brigid, Columcille, and Brendan, along with those lesser known beyond the borders of Ireland such as Gobnait, Ita, Kevin, Enda, Colman, Dearbhla, Sourney, and Ciaran. While the Celtic tradition extends to areas in Great Britain including Scotland and Wales, I have decided to focus my own exploration on Ireland, my adopted homeland.

As in some of my previous books, my husband, John, also offers reflections in each chapter on scripture texts that relate to the theme. You will also be invited in each chapter to explore the concepts presented through the creative arts, specifically through photography and writing. Photography can provide a way to see the world more deeply and receive the gifts freely offered to us. Prompts for exploring through writing can draw you into poetic forms for expression. Throughout the book, you will also find invitations to contemplative walks with specific themes and points of focus.

This is a book for those of you exploring alternate ways of discerning your path, one that honors the moment-by-moment invitations offered and your soul's seasonal rhythms and one that feels more in alignment with your creative spirit.

This is not meant to be a systematic, step-by-step book but rather an invitation into a set of practices and ways of being in the world that support us in listening for our own organic unfolding. When we allow ourselves to ripen, our lives become all the sweeter, and we discover a way ahead that is in deep alignment with our souls.

You can read this book through, but also feel free to skip around the chapters, beginning with one that especially draws you first. This is part of the practice, to learn to trust what kindles your heart and follow that to see where it leads.

I always recommend reading these kinds of books slowly. They are meant to be practiced and integrated over time. Gather a small group of kindred souls to explore the practices and creative explorations together. You could move through the book over twelve weeks or even twelve months to let the materials and practices be integrated slowly.

May the journey ahead be rich and full of holy surprises.

chapter 1

The practice of Thresholds

Thresholds were important to the ancient Irish monks whose wisdom guides us on this path. Thresholds are the space between, when we move from one time to another, as in the threshold of dawn to day or of dusk to dark; one space to another, as in times of inner or outer journeying or pilgrimage; and one awareness to another, as in times when our old structures start to fall away and we begin to build something new. The Celts describe thresholds as "thin times or places" where heaven and earth are closer together and the veil between worlds is thin.

In the Celtic imagination, thresholds are potent places. We experience the thresholds of the year unfolding, so that each new season beckons us into a renewed awareness of the nearness of the holy presence. In the Celtic wheel of the year there are eight portals in time that mark the equinoxes and solstices, as well as the midway points between them. Each of these festivals held the possibility of deeper connection to the divine. We will explore this further in chapter 10.

We encounter thresholds each day through the movement across the hinges of time. The turning of early morning and evening were thought to be especially graced times of day when the otherworld was near.

There are physical places that evoke a sense of wonder. My husband, John, wonders if "thin places" means they were worn thin by the many souls who have been drawn to these liminal landscapes and sought prayer there. When we lead pilgrimages together in Ireland, there is a keen sense in the holy sites we visit of the thousands of prayers that have washed over the place.

The ancient Celts used to have "threshold stones" at the entrance to a sacred site, one on either side of the portal or passageway. (We still find this tradition alive in many of the monastic ruins as well.) The stones were markers and reminders that the soul was crossing over into a sanctified space. In many of these places, churches were later built, which shows a continuity of awareness of sacred places.

Philip Sheldrake writes that the Celtic peoples had "a fascination for the spiritual quality of boundary places. Living on physical boundaries also symbolized a state of liminality—of living literally and spiritually on the margins or between worlds, the material one and the spiritual one."[1] The monks were drawn to edge places, inspired by monks before them who had fled to the desert. The Celtic Church grew on the very borders of civilization, at the outer edge of Europe and beyond much of the reach of the Roman Empire. In a seventh-century letter to Pope Boniface IV, St. Columbanus described his people as *ultimi habitatores mundi*, "inhabitants of the world's edge."[2] They lived at the very fringes of the ancient world and embraced the perspective it gave them.

I love this image and wonder what it would mean for each of us to claim that identity. What does it mean to be an inhabitant of the world's edge? To go out to wild threshold places, into the holy darkness, and embrace a fertile and wide expanse of possibility there beyond the safe constructs of culture and the expectations that slowly suffocate our creative hearts?

We encounter thresholds in our experience as well—those times when life shifts, sometimes out of choice, and often because of circumstance. My mother's death in 2003 was a huge threshold in my life not of my choosing, while John and my move to Europe in 2012 was a deliberate choice. Both were extraordinarily challenging, each in their own ways and full of their own kind of grace.

Thresholds and Discernment

If you are in a place of discernment in your life, a season of pondering next steps, then you are on a threshold as well. Thresholds are liminal times when the past season has come to a close but there is a profound unknowing of what will come next.

The Celtic monks were deeply influenced by the stories of the desert mothers and fathers. There is a wonderful story from St. Anthony that goes like this: "Abba Antony said to Abba Joseph, 'How would you explain this saying?' and he replied, 'I do not know.' Then Abba Anthony said, 'Indeed, Abba Joseph has found the way, for he has said: "I do not know.""[3]

"I do not know," and "[He] has found the way." We are invited to release everything to which we cling too tightly: our need to be right, our need to feel secure, our need to be in control. None of those is the way according to the desert and Celtic monks.

Thresholds are challenging because they demand that we step into the in-between place of letting go of what has been while awaiting what is still to come. When we are able to fully release our need to control the outcome, thresholds become rich and graced places of transformation. We can only become something new when we have released the old faces we have been wearing, even if it means not knowing quite who we are in the space between.

Thresholds are as much imaginal places as they are literal and physical ones. The Celtic imagination saw this liminal place alive within us. Dolores Whelan writes, "The imaginal world is the region between the physical or material world and the spiritual world or ultimate mystery or source. This is the Celtic otherworld, Tír na nÓg, also known as the *mundus imaginalis* of the Celts. This otherworld is not an archetype produced by the unconscious mind, nor is it a product of fictional imagination. It is a dimension of reality that exists within the world and with the psyche or soul, the inner dimension of self."[4]

As spiritual seekers, we are called to live with one foot in the world of earthly and everyday experience. The other foot is in the transcendent realm where the divine breaks through our ordinary consciousness. To hold this kind of imaginal awareness is to recognize heaven on earth and the kingdom breaking through in each moment.

When we are in discernment, it means keeping an eye attuned to the ways that the holy touches us through experience. We can cultivate the capacity to see another layer of reality at work. We can listen for symbols and encounters with this numinousness because it happens within the very deepest recesses of our souls. To allow the soul's slow ripening asks that we sit in the mystery, at times on the threshold, awaiting the moment of fullness.

St. Brigid of Kildare

In Ireland, Brigid is one of the three patron saints of the land, alongside Patrick and Columba. We don't know many details of her life, and there is great evidence that she is part of a much older lineage extending back to the Irish triple goddess Brigid of pre-Christian times who was the goddess of poets, smithwork, and healing.

The saint is said to have been born on a threshold. Her mother was standing, straddling a doorway, when Brigid came into her earthly form. There is a tradition from this of midwives calling upon the presence of Brigid at the time of birth, honoring her reality as a midwife of the threshold place.

Most of what we know about St. Brigid comes from *Life of Brigid*, written by the monk Cogitosis in the second half of the seventh century. *Life* emphasizes her healing, her kinship with animals, her profound sense of hospitality and generosity, and her concern for those oppressed. These stories of the saints are not meant to be literal or historical but spiritual, mythical, archetypal, and psychological, resonating with the deepest parts of our souls.

Her feast day is February 1, which in the Celtic calendar is also the feast of Imbolc and the threshold into springtime. It is the time when the ewes begin to give birth and give forth their milk, and it heralds the coming of longer and warmer days. Brigid is believed to bring the first sign of life after the long, dark nights of winter. She breathes into the landscape so that it begins to awaken. Snowdrops, the first flowers of spring, are one of her symbols.

Often in Ireland, I have heard Brigid described as a bridge between the pre-Christian and Christian traditions, between the other world and this one. She bridges the thresholds between traditions and draws them together under her mantle.

Consider calling upon Brigid each morning of the coming days, asking her to help you tend the threshold of your life right now.

Scripture Reflection by John Valters Paintner

Lectio Divina

Each chapter will have a scripture passage that you will be invited to pray with in the ancient practice of lectio divina. *Lectio divina* means "sacred reading" and is an ancient, contemplative way of praying with sacred texts that is practiced in monastic communities. Lectio asks us to release our desire to have something happen or know what a text means for us and to drop down into our intuitive sense and wait to receive whatever gifts may be offered to us. If you are unfamiliar with this way of praying, please refer to the guidelines in the appendix and apply those guidelines to your reading of this passage:

> Thus says the LORD:
> Stand at the crossroads, and look,
>   and ask for the ancient paths,
> where the good way lies; and walk in it,
>   and find rest for your souls.
>   —Jeremiah 6:16

Biblical Context

The prophet Jeremiah grew up during the religious reforms of the good King Josiah. The Book of the Law had been rediscovered, and with the help of the prophetess Hulda, the people of Judah were returning to the covenant and to God. It was a time of great spiritual renewal and hope for the Chosen People.

But then King Josiah died in battle against the Egyptians and the reforms were thrown out with the new king. (Fortunately, the religious movement started by King Josiah did continue. During the Babylonian Exile, the followers of these reforms became known as the Deuteronomists and were responsible not only for writing the book of Deuteronomy but also compiling and editing most of what we think of today as the Old Testament.)

Jeremiah recognized that Josiah's movement was the last chance to avoid the judgment of God. The Chosen People had broken the covenant for too long, and the consequences were going to be disastrous. Jeremiah envisioned the total destruction of the kingdom. Nothing would be left intact, and everyone would be affected. While some prophets wrote to warn the people from impending doom and destruction, Jeremiah was both pessimistic and hopeful. He was pessimistic in that, with the death of Josiah, Jeremiah believed that the punishment of Judah was inevitable. And yet he still preached. His hope was not in the immediate future but in an age to come. He hoped that some would survive. He hoped that they would look back on all that had happened and realize their mistakes so they could restore the covenant with God. One gets the sense that this was more a hope of Jeremiah's rather than faith in its certainty.

Jeremiah did not live to see the covenant restored. But his teachings became a cornerstone to the slow rebuilding of faith among God's people. In his words, the exiles found important lessons that led them back to God and the Promised Land. The book Jeremiah left behind became an important aid to learning from the mistakes of the past and discerning the path ahead.

In Jeremiah 6:16, Jeremiah warns the Israelites that they stand at the threshold of a new era. There is a crossroad before them, and they must choose the correct path. Staying where they are is not an option. Their enemies are in pursuit. Staying put means death. To live, one must move.

Not every journey, whether physical or spiritual, is intended. The people of Judah had no intention of going anywhere. They were quite comfortable with their lives, too comfortable. When Jeremiah confronted them about their transgressions against God and one another, they refused to be moved. But their misdeeds and their stubbornness forced a change.

They failed to see the threshold they were standing on, even as the prophet pointed it out. When the Exile came, they had wasted their chance to stop and consider their options. Fortunately, for those who survived, they had the words of Jeremiah to comfort and guide them.

Personal Reflection

Have you ever entered a room and suddenly realized that you've completely forgotten why you were there? (Be honest; I know I'm not alone on this one.) Well, don't panic. There may be a perfectly reasonable and comforting explanation for it.

A recent scientific theory going around is that it's not just a "senior moment." It very well may be a normal brain function. When we walk across a threshold, a door or other barrier of some kind, our subconscious minds recognize that we are going from one environment to another. To prepare us for the possible dangers of a new space, our brains do a quick short-term memory dump in order to free up more active cerebral computing space so we can more quickly adapt and react to whatever we may encounter.

You aren't losing your mind. It's an evolutionary adaptation that allowed your ancestors to survive and you to be here now.

In hindsight, there were plenty of warning signs that my time at the high school I taught at in Seattle was nearing an end. I just wasn't ready to see them. I appreciated the blessing of teaching (and learning about) a subject I love: Hebrew Scriptures. I worked with many great people, and most of the students were delightful.

But there were conflicts; there were struggles. I tried overlooking them. It just made matters worse.

So when the subject I loved was pulled out from under me, I could no longer ignore that I was being driven from my comfortable (if not completely perfect) home. I was at a crossroads that I did not ask for. I didn't want to be there. I wanted things to stay the same.

But life is movement. Life is change.

And so I quit my job, we sold our home and most of our belongings, and we traveled to Europe. We became exiles, strangers in a strange land. And it was good.

I needed the change. It was time. But it could easily have been nothing more than a long vacation or retreat from reality, leaving everything behind and forgetting all my problems. But I used our time living in Vienna as an opportunity to look back and reflect. I took time to stand on the threshold, consider, and learn from the past before moving forward. It is an ongoing journey, but the threshold demands reflection and openness.

Now living in Ireland, I have discovered new possibilities beyond my imagining. We have settled in a city with a vibrant theater and film culture, both of which are passions of mine. I now have time to write—short stories and plays and film scripts—and am involved with a wonderful community of people who support one another in bringing these to life. When we stand at the threshold, we can't possibly know what awaits us.

The Practice of Thresholds

In the days ahead, become aware of all the times you cross a threshold. This might be moving from one space to another—entering through a doorway, transitioning from one activity to the next, or tending the thresholds of the day, especially at dawn and dusk. Pause at each and offer a short blessing, simply becoming aware of the possibilities alive in the moment. See if the threshold helps call forth the thinness of this moment, making the voice of the divine more accessible.

Reading this book and taking on its practices is a threshold experience, inviting you to an inner journeying from old patterns into renewed commitments to intimacy with God. It is about a shift in awareness as you seek to embrace a new vision.

Wander out to edge places—the threshold of shoreline, where forests begin, or borders between towns—and ponder those thresholds within you. Bless each threshold you cross, that you might remember to hold loosely all that you think you know.

We are forever crossing thresholds in our lives, both the literal kind when moving through doorways, leaving a building, or passing into another room, and the metaphorical thresholds, when time becomes a transition space of waiting and tending. We hope for news about a friend struggling with illness; we long for clarity about our own deepest dreams.

In the monastic tradition, *statio* is the practice of stopping one thing before beginning another. It is the acknowledgment that in the space of transition and threshold is a sacred dimension, a holy pause full of possibility. This place between is a place of stillness, where we let go of what came before and prepare ourselves to enter fully into what comes next.

When we pause between activities or spaces or moments in our days, we open ourselves to the possibility of discovering a new kind of presence to the darkness of in-between times. When we rush from one thing to another, we skim over the surface of life, losing the sacred attentiveness that brings forth revelations in the most ordinary of moments.

Statio calls us to a sense of reverence for slowness, for mindfulness, and for the fertile dark spaces between our goals where we can pause and center ourselves, and listen. We can open up a space within for God to work. We can become fully conscious of what we are about to do rather than mindlessly completing another task.

We often think of these in-between times as wasted moments and inconveniences, rather than opportunities to return again and again, to awaken to the gifts right here, not the ones we imagine waiting for us beyond the next door.

Photography Exploration: Thresholds

In each chapter of this book, I will invite you to go on a contemplative walk. There are some simple guidelines for this in the appendix. Essentially, this is a walk where you aren't trying to get anywhere but simply striving to pay attention step by step to what calls to you.

During your walk, use your camera to receive images that deepen your experience. In my book *Eyes of the Heart: Photography as a Contemplative Practice*, I write about the difference between "taking" photos and "receiving" them. The first is reflective of our consumerist, grasping, scarcity-focused mindset, so prevalent in Western culture. The second is the call of the monk, the contemplative, the one in us who sees all of life as gift and so receives the graces offered with a sense of wonder and gratitude. It is the difference between walking around with closed fists or open palms. Open your hands wide and pay attention to what gifts and graces arrive when we move through the world in an open-hearted way. The frame of the lens helps you to see them in new ways and reflect again later on what you have encountered.

Your invitation is to walk and be open to noticing all the places of threshold you discover: doorways, gates, transition places from one kind of space to another, such as the transition from home to work or from city to countryside. See what you notice as you bring this awareness with you. As you encounter each threshold, use your camera to receive an image of it to carry with you. Notice which thresholds especially stir your heart.

When you return home, see if one of these images speaks to your heart and rest with it a while. What might it reveal about the threshold you are standing on in your own life?

Writing Exploration: Three Questions

In addition to photography, I will also invite you in each chapter into some written exploration. These exercises are meant to simply open up your curiosity and inquiry and see where the writing leads you.

As we begin the journey of this book, consider what questions you carry with you. If you are in discernment, what are the graces your heart is seeking?

Phil Cousineau, author of *The Art of Pilgrimage*, describes questions as the beginning of a quest, and the poet Rainer Maria Rilke invites us to "live the questions" as a way of dwelling in mystery. Questions point us to thresholds of unknowing. They might be sparked by awareness of our own mortality and the preciousness of days or the grace of thresholds all around us.

Do some free writing and listen for three questions you can bring to this time of reading and praying with this book. Write them down in a journal and number them 1, 2, and 3.

Everything is always an invitation. However, we will work with the three questions toward the end of this book, so allowing space for them now will deepen that experience later.

Closing Blessing

We come to the close of our chapter on the practice of thresholds. I am hopeful you have become more keenly aware of all the ways thresholds in time and space impact your daily life and how holding more awareness of these moments can offer a gift of possibility. What are you discovering about your own thresholds?

As a closing blessing, I offer this poem I wrote about St. Brigid—based on a legend that her tears over the suffering of the world fell to the ground and there grew a fruit tree. Brigid is the patron of thresholds, and in this story, I hear the threshold between sorrow and new life, between honoring grief and opening to possibilities.

st. Brigid and the fruit tree

There was the moment
you could bear it no more.
Your eyes brimming with
great glistening drops
summoned by the hunger of
the world, the callous and
terrible things men and
women do to one another.

Your tears splashed onto
cold stony earth, ringing out
like bells calling monks to prayer,

like the river breaking open to
the wide expanse of sea.

From that salt-soaked ground
a fruit tree sprouts and rises.
I imagine pendulous pears,
tears transmuted to sweetness.

There will always be more grief
than we can bear.
There will always be ripe fruit flesh
making your fingers sticky from the juice.

Life is tidal, rising and receding,
its long loneliness, its lush loveliness,
no need to wish for low tide when
the banks are breaking.

The woman in labor straddles the doorway
screaming out your name.
You stand there on the threshold, weeping,

and pear trees still burst into blossom,
their branches hang so heavy, low,
you don't even have to reach.[5]

chapter 2

The practice of Dreaming

In ancient times, dreams were respected as signs from God, invitations to a calling bigger than what we might imagine in our waking lives and the limits of daylight vision. Dreams can be vital to pay attention to during times of discernment, as they give clues and indications of the soul's unique gifts and longings. They can help to support each of us in our *yes* to a life that is uniquely our own, to say yes to the gifts which can only be birthed through us.

Dreams play a significant role in scripture, with guidance and direction often arriving in these night visions. From Joseph of the Old Testament (see Genesis 37:1–34), Jacob's dream of a staircase from earth to heaven with angels ascending and descending (see Genesis 28:10–17), and Daniel's dream of the four beasts (see Daniel 7:1–14) to Joseph of the New Testament having four separate dreams that are recalled in the gospels—being told not to be afraid to take pregnant Mary as his wife (see Matthew 1:20–21), being warned to leave Bethlehem and flee to Egypt (see Matthew 2:13), later being told that it is safe to go back to Israel (see Matthew 2:19–20), and then being instructed to depart for the region of Galilee instead of going to Judea (see Matthew 2:22)—God regularly appears to people through their dreams, offering important messages.

We have the dreams of many Celtic saints recorded as well. St. Patrick is said to have had a dream where he was visited by an angel who encouraged him to flee his captivity and helped arrange a miraculous escape. Later he had a dream where he heard the Irish people calling out to him to return to the land of his enslavement.

In a story about St. Brigid as a young girl, a Druid had a dream in which he saw three clerics anoint her with oil and was told that her name would be St. Brigid. Later, a bishop of her time had a dream about Brigid in which she appeared as Mary. In the sixth century, Brigid began to be referred to as "Mary of the Gaels."

St. David, a sixth-century Welsh bishop, is said to have had a dream in which he found three gifts: a stag, a fish, and a beehive that predicted his life path. The honeycomb symbolized wisdom; the fish, self-denial; and the stag, his power over the serpent.

Just as in the biblical texts, dreams are one of the primary ways God speaks to the Celtic monks and reveals new directions and ways to them. Often they happen at threshold times when a monk is being called forth to something new.

Dreams continue to call us into ways of being that are less linear and more intuitive, less goal-driven and more open to receiving the gifts being offered to us in the moment. Our own dreams may seem much less straightforward than these biblical and saintly dreams. They speak a language that can feel confusing to our waking minds, so we must approach with reverence and hospitality. There is a grace offered in listening to their wisdom.

Dreams and Discernment

All of the great Celtic harvest festivals begin with a celebration the night before. The feast of Christmas begins with the evening prior; Easter morning actually starts at Easter vigil. All Hallow's Eve begins the honoring of All Saint's Day. Daily monastic prayers begin with vigils, early in the morning, before light has emerged into the sky. Similarly, traditions that have lunar calendars begin with the new moon, when the moon is in darkness.

These reminders that everything begins in darkness and emerges from the night, much like the great womb of our own birthing, offer some solace and courage to welcome in the darkness in our lives. We might, perhaps, begin to see the fertile space of new life alongside the uncertainties and fears. The invitation is to trust that in the great holy night, the "treasures of darkness" of which the prophet Isaiah writes truly exist. In these dark hours, our dreams arrive like gifts of insight and direction.

The darkness is holy because, as the monks teach us, everything bears holiness, everything can be the occasion for revelation—even the deepest grief or the darkest uncertainties. The darkness brings forth our dream wisdom.

Thresholds can feel like dark places, and discernment means we are in the midst of unknowing. As John and I moved through our midlife adventure, dreams became my close companion as I looked to them to help discern how we were being called. I wrote down whatever snippets I could remember to work with the images in my waking life, both on my own and with my spiritual director. They acted like a trail of breadcrumbs out of the darkness and into illumination.

St. Ciaran and His Dream

St. Ciaran lived in the sixth century and is one of the great monastic founders known as the "Twelve Apostles of Ireland." Ciaran went out to the island of Inishmore to spend time with Abbott Enda, who was a great leader in the monastic community of Ireland. There they both had a dream of a great, fruitful tree growing beside a stream in the middle of Ireland. In the vision, they could see the tree protecting the entire island with abundant fruit provided.

Enda said that the tree is a symbol of Ciaran and how he had grown great in the eyes of God and the people. He said that Ireland would be protected and sheltered by Ciaran's grace, and he would nourish others by his presence and prayers. Enda then told Ciaran to go to the very center of Ireland and build his church on the banks of the river stream. I love this great and flourishing tree as a symbol of Ciaran's call in life. He was moving toward his own soul's ripening. The dream pointed the way.

He founded his monastery at the intersection of the river Shannon running north to south and the esker, a system of ridges forming a natural roadway, which runs across Ireland from east to west. The monastery, Clonmacnoise, became one of the largest and most significant monasteries of the entire Irish Church as a center of learning.

Call upon St. Ciaran in the days ahead to help you remember your night dreams and to guide you in interpreting God's invitation to you through them.

Scripture Reflection by John Valters Paintner

Lectio Divina

> Now after they had left, an angel of the Lord appeared to Joseph in a dream and said, "Get up, take the child and his mother, and flee to Egypt, and remain there until I tell you; for Herod is about to search for the child, to destroy him." Then Joseph got up, took the child and his mother by night, and went to Egypt, and remained there until the death of Herod. This was to fulfill what had been spoken by the Lord through the prophet, "Out of Egypt I have called my son."
> —Matthew 2:13–15

Biblical Context

I want to begin with Joseph of the Hebrew Scriptures. At just seventeen, Joseph was the youngest of Jacob's many sons. Not only was he his father's favorite (parents of the Bible tend to play favorites and not even try to hide it), but he was blessed with a great gift: dreams. Young, arrogant Joseph—already on his siblings' bad side for being their father's spy, who reported about his brothers' bad work—did himself no favors when he told his family of his dream.

In a dream, God foretold to Joseph that his family would bow down to him one day, which Joseph then tells to his family. To make matters worse, Joseph even tells his father that he too will bow down to him. In retaliation, Joseph's brothers sell him into slavery and tell Jacob that he is dead.

But enslaved and imprisoned in Egypt, Joseph's gift of dreams saved him. Joseph interpreted the dreams of his fellow prisoners, which later brought him to the attention of the Pharaoh, who also suffered from troubling dreams. Joseph interpreted a dream, easing Pharaoh's anxiety and helping the Egyptians prepare for the seven-year famine that would come. This same famine affected Joseph's family back in the Promised Land, who came to Egypt for help. Joseph's dream ultimately saved and reunited his family.

In the gospels, Mary's husband, Joseph, also was blessed to receive divine messages through dreams. First, when he learned of Mary's pregnancy, an angel reassured him and so Joseph married Mary and raised Jesus. What faith it must have taken for this humble man, who had already resigned himself to quietly divorcing Mary, to accept that his wife-to-be's unborn child was not just special but divinely so! The Bible is full of women "being with child" through miraculous means. And though I'm sure Joseph was familiar with all those stories of long ago, to find himself in the midst of such a story . . . he could have easily ignored the dream entirely and gone back to his simple life. Instead, Joseph said yes to the dream's message—and so the story continues.

In another dream, shortly after the birth of Jesus, an angel warned Joseph of Herod's wicked plans. Under divine guidance, thanks to the dream, Joseph took the Holy Family to Egypt to escape persecution. I think what often gets overlooked here is that it must have been much easier for Joseph to accept this second dream's message. He must have begun to look forward to his dreams and the guidance they would bring.

Personal Reflection

Many years ago, when we lived in the Bay Area, Christine and I participated in a thirty-week version of the Spiritual Exercises of St. Ignatius. Six of us met once a week for group spiritual direction. Each week we had a different theme or question. One of the weeks was focused on what God was asking of us. During that week, I had the most profound dream.

The dream began simply enough. I was walking along the sidewalk near our apartment at the time in San Francisco, near Golden Gate Park. But then, as dreams go, things got weird. An adult male African elephant (I could tell, somehow, by the size of the ears and tusks) was rampaging through the city streets. Even as it began to chase me, I was yelling at people, trying to warn them of the imminent danger. But nobody else seemed to be all that concerned. I remember grabbing someone by the lapels and pleading with him to run and hide someplace safe. He brushed me off and said matter-of-factly, "Why? It's not chasing *me*."

That's when I realized that the elephant was only after me. I ran, but the elephant was faster. I climbed trees, only to have the elephant knock them down. I climbed metal utility poles, only to have the elephant bend and snap them to the ground. I ducked into buildings, only to have the elephant smash through the walls. The elephant was relentless. Just as it got its trunk around my leg to yank me to the ground, I awoke with a start . . . and a realization.

The message of the dream was as clear to me as the details themselves: God (the elephant) was pursuing me and nothing would stop that pursuit. I wasn't sure what God wanted, but I knew there was no running and no hiding from God.

Another time I felt God was speaking through me in a dream was while I was chaperoning a weekend retreat for the high school where I was a teacher. Students had been asked to leave their cell phones at home. Knowing this had likely not happened, during the opening orientation the leaders asked the retreatants to turn their phones off and put them away for the duration of the retreat. There were even threats of confiscation made, but it was all for naught.

I had been on several such retreats with the school, and they had all been positive experiences. There were always a few students who tried to sneak a call or a couple of text messages, but not like on that retreat. Even after several students had their phones confiscated, the mobile mayhem continued.

And it was just day two of a four-night retreat.

But that night I awoke from a dream at midnight, thanks to a cell-phone alarm going off. (Ironically, it belonged to the one student who had actually turned his phone off and put it in the bottom of his bag. Unfortunately, in shoving it in his bag, he had accidently turned it back on and the alarm was automatically set.) Thanks to the cheap, thin construction of the cabins, everyone woke up. But while others woke up annoyed (or in the case of the one student: embarrassed and very apologetic), I woke up with a scripture story running through my head.

Maybe it was because I had just been teaching about 1 Kings 19, but the story of Elijah's flight to Mount Horeb was all I could think about. In the tale, Elijah is on the run from King Ahab and Queen Jezebel, who are determined to kill him. The prophet is told to climb the sacred mountain and await God's presence.

First a strong, rock-crushing wind sweeps over the mountain. Next an earthquake shakes the earth where Elijah stands. Then a fire rages. And yet, God was not present in any of these events, which we still categorize as "acts of God."

It was only in the silence that followed that Elijah heard a tiny, whispering sound. The prophet hid his face in his cloak, for he felt God's presence in the quiet.

I knew I had to tell the retreatants this story. I knew I had to remind them of the importance of silence, of how distracting noise can be in our holy pursuits. And I knew I had to ask them the same question God asked Elijah: Why are you here?

What do the scriptures reveal to you about the importance of listening to dreams? Why are you here?

The Practice of Remembering Dreams

If you usually can't remember your dreams, one of the best ways to invite memory is to place a journal and a pen by your bed at night before sleeping and then ask God for a dream. Even if you awaken with only a fragment or a feeling, record that upon waking. Honor whatever comes, and be aware when you dismiss dream images because you think they are too mundane or strange.

Write your own blessing for the gifts that holy darkness can bring. Bless the rich, fertile soil from which new life emerges, the womb-space where all birthing begins. Write an invocation that calls for the wisdom of dreams to bless you in the night.

Bless the wild edges of life where safe conventions are stripped away and space is opened for new imaginings. Bless the thresholds that signal the movement from one understanding to another. Bless the holy pauses and moments when each of us can rest into what has been and prepare for what will come.

I find it most helpful to write down the dream in present tense, so as not to distance myself from it, and to give it a title. Each of the characters or symbols that appears represents an aspect of ourselves. Often the more fearful elements of a dream are parts of our shadow selves that have not yet been integrated.

It can also help to write the dream down in symbols or visual language—so as you write out the narrative, when you come to something that could be depicted with a simple symbol, draw that instead of the writing a word. Another helpful tool is not necessarily writing your dream from left to right in a linear way, as you might when journaling. Write the dream in a spiral, or sideways in your notebook, or upside down on the page. This signals to the mind that you are not working with linear restrictions.

Choose one character or dream symbol to begin. Write from the perspective of this image—begin with "I am" and speak from the voice of this energy. How does it experience the world? What is it like to see through this particular lens?

After you have written for a while, the next step is to embody the dream character. Take a few moments to center yourself and connect with your breath; bring this energy into your body and see how it feels. How does this character or symbol move through the world? What gestures or postures might it take? Explore for several minutes the different physical possibilities.

Try this for several dream symbols and then enter them into a dialogue with one another, either on paper through writing or by moving back and forth physically between the embodied energies. Consider what you discover.

Stephen Aizenstat, a Jungian analyst and author of *Dream Tending*, draws on three key questions that help to animate dream images and understand their deeper message:

Who is visiting now?

What's happening here?

What is the dream's desire?

When we descend into the holy darkness of night and receive an invitation through symbol and imagery, we are called to trust in the imagination of a God much bigger than ourselves.

Photography Exploration: Taking a Dream for a Walk

You are invited again on a contemplative walk. Bring a dream you had one night with you as you walk. Imagine that you are walking through the dream again as you move through the world. Notice if there are moments around you shimmering in response. See if any symbols that present themselves either deepen the dream's meaning or allow it to unfold further.

Approach this time as if it were a dream, meaning that you allow things to unfold and stay present without trying to direct what happens.

If you aren't remembering your own dreams, you could also bring one of the dreams from the scriptures we explored earlier or one of the dreams of the Celtic saints. Imagine walking with Ciaran's dream of the great tree by the river and see what you notice and discover.

Several years ago I had a series of dreams about a cello. One morning I went for a walk in my Seattle neighborhood and went around my usual route, which passed a college for the arts. On that morning after my third cello dream, I saw a woman playing cello out on the front lawn, practicing. It was mid-October and chilly. I was stunned.

What synchronicities does the world offer to you? Let yourself be with the images received in a prayerful way, listening for their wisdom.

Writing Exploration: Upon Awakening

Keep a journal by your bed, and every morning when you wake, make a commitment to write whatever comes to mind, for ten to fifteen minutes without editing or stopping. It may be a particular dream that you had or it may be just a feeling or image you are aware of. Some mornings may feel cloudy with confusion; you can write about that. Do this writing exploration before you check your email or social media, before you talk to anyone else. You want to dwell in that in-between space between sleep and wakefulness and honor whatever you notice there. These little tidbits may seem meaningless some mornings, and some days you may start to see patterns and new insights revealed. This practice is valuable even if you do not remember your dreams.

Closing Blessing

I hope your dreams will be generous. If not, have patience and keep showing up to receive them. Remember that everything is a practice, one that calls us to a lifetime of embodying this way of being.

I offer in closing a poem I wrote about St. Ciaran's dream. Perhaps read it through twice and see what shimmers forth for you. Blessings upon your dreams! May the One who is revealed in both light and dark show you the rich, fertile soil of night vision.

st. ciaran and the dream

Scent of morning startles
Ciaran awake from his dream.
All that lingers is the silver river
that runs through the fallow field
of his mind, banks swerving around

an opulent oak, brown antiphon of swallows
singing praises, saying *here*.

Hunger of daylight becomes his compass.
Overhead, blue vaults the umber earth
as he follows veins of quartz across granite—
an atlas of the heart—
until he finds the river rushing
and he rests under the glorious tree
and breathes fully, finally free.

chapter 3

The practice of *peregrinatio* and seeking your place of resurrection

For the Celtic monastic tradition, wandering was a powerful practice, shaping much of their vision of Christian spiritual life. There is a unique term for this Celtic wandering—*peregrinatio pro Christo*—the call to wander for the love of Christ. It is a phrase without precise definition in English and that means something different than pilgrimage. This wandering is an invitation to let go of our own agendas and discover where God is leading.

The wandering saints set forth without destination—often getting into small boats with no oars or rudder, called coracles—and trusted themselves to "the currents of divine love." They surrendered themselves completely to elements of wind and ocean. The river or sea would bring them to places of rest that they had not chosen themselves. The impulse for the journeys was always love.

In this profound practice, God becomes both destination and way, companion and guiding force. God is in the call to the journey and the unfolding of the journey, and God greets us at the journey's end. The goal of this wandering is always to find the place of our resurrection, the place where our gifts can be brought fully to life for the rest of our days. Sometimes a monk will arrive somewhere and think he or she has found it, only to be later called by God to move on once more.

The story of Abram is the source of inspiration for this Celtic understanding of *peregrinatio*. Abram was called to leave his home and go to a place he would be shown. He would later change his name to Abraham as a sign of this calling. "By faith Abraham obeyed when he was called to set out for a place that he was to receive as an inheritance; and he set out, not knowing where he was going" (Heb 11:8). The Celtic monks were inspired by this story, and they depicted it in many places in their artwork, as well as interpreting the command to "go forth" as personally addressing them: "St. Columba is reputed to have said in a sermon: God counseled Abraham to leave his own country and go in pilgrimage into the land which God had shown him, to wit the 'Land of Promise'—Now the good counsel which God enjoined here on the father of the faithful is incumbent on all the faithful; that is to leave their country and their land, their wealth and their worldly delight for the sake of the Lord of the Elements, and go in perfect pilgrimage in imitation of Him."[1]

The goal was always to surrender to God's direction and be led to the place of resurrection, which was equivalent to the promised land of Abraham. Theologian Philip Sheldrake describes this: "The journey of wandering ascetics was actually a search for the ultimate place, a place of harmony and the unity of all things in the Absolute."[2]

Modern Celtic monk Dara Molloy, who lives on the island of Inishmore and is one of our pilgrimage guides, describes it as more "a destiny than a destination." The seekers believed truly that there was a place they were called to be and following the signs God gave them would lead them there. It was the place where they would flourish and also the place of their death and eventual resurrection into new life.

Most of the stories we have of the Irish saints offer examples of these calls to wander until they found their own true places. Many of these calls happened through dreams. All the journeys involved crossing thresholds into the unknown.

Peregrinatio and Discernment

After John and I sold everything we owned and traveled in 2012 to Vienna to live, we eventually felt the call to move to Ireland. Vienna is a city I love dearly, but there were many obstacles that arose in our time living there, mainly involving the immigration process for John. Even though I have Austrian citizenship through my father, applying for John's residency grew more and more challenging. It became clear this was the not the place where we were being called to put down roots. There were many layers to this choice, but above all, we sensed that Ireland was inviting us to dwell in her landscape without fully knowing why.

Many people were surprised by this shift of direction, but I can look back and see clearly the movement of the Spirit at work, calling us to a place where our souls and our work could be nourished in ways we couldn't have imagined. This is why the first impulse is always love. At the time it felt like another great journey of trust and yielding to the currents carrying us forward as well as a huge challenge to move and start over once again. Now that we have been in Galway for five years, we feel something very powerful at work that we continue to discover unfolding.

I remember soon after moving to Galway, we traveled out to the island of Inishmore to first meet Dara Molloy, a wonderful guide and Celtic priest who now helps lead our pilgrimage days out to the island and who also led our ritual renewal of vows for our twentieth anniversary in 2014.

Dara shared some of his life's journey and his own experience of *peregrinatio*, how after living most of his life in Dublin ministering as a Catholic priest, he arrived on Inishmore for a time of retreat and solitude, and he felt he had come home. I recognized myself in his story and the stories of Irish monks seeking out their hearts' true landscape. I could see how John and I had set out for Vienna hoping that would be where we found our home, but that was not to be. I fell even more deeply in love with Vienna, but we were carried on to Ireland, another place that had always called to our hearts.

I am not able to say yet with certainty that this is our place of resurrection, but it continues to feel more and more true. That is part of the invitation of living in threshold spaces. But perhaps that is not as important as staying true to the current and where it wants to carry us. We try to keep our hearts aligned with the winds of the Spirit.

One of my favorite lines of poetry comes from Antonio Machado: "wanderer, there is no road / the way is made by walking."[3] The Christian scriptures speak of a "way," but it is not the path of our expectations. It is not the ten-step plan for inner peace. Instead, this way calls us to a deeper and more radical trust and to realize that the way is made by walking. Each step is shaped by listening to how the divine presence calls us forward, the direction we take, the choices we make, and how much control we are willing to yield.

As we deepen into paying attention to what this moment actually brings, we can then begin to follow how one moment unfolds from another.

How do we practice *peregrinatio* in the modern world, where stepping into a rudderless boat without oars seems dangerous and impractical? How do we know when we are following the divine current?

Abba Poemen, one of the desert fathers, is credited with this saying: "Do not give your heart to that which does not satisfy your heart."[4]

This is a very simple phrase, but powerful in its application. Said in the positive, only give your heart to that which satisfies your heart. I am called each day to reflect on what I did and experienced that was deeply life-giving. When I follow that way, I know that each step is blessed. How many days do I come to prayer and realize how much I have battled myself within? Or followed a trail that I knew did not lead toward life? And yet gentleness with ourselves is also a part of this heart-nourishing way.

John will reflect on the biblical story of the call of Abraham and Sarah. When John and I prayed with the text, the words that shimmered for me were "walk before me."

I sat with that image for a long while. It didn't say "come follow me" or "I will guide you." The text invited them, and me, to walk *before* God. I let the image dwell in me until I saw the boats the Irish monks stepped into and I felt the current and wind come from behind to push them toward their destination. It is a more subtle kind of practice, one where we have to lean back and feel where the wind and current are guiding us. We must lean in a holy direction.

We need to step out and feel the way, how the Spirit guides. The wind and current come from behind to usher us forward. God is saying we must walk first, not follow, and feel the allure of the Spirit along the way, to trust that the fresh perspective will come as a wind or current from behind. We know this when we respond to what deeply nourishes the heart.

I think, too, of how Abram and Sarai received new names and how this is part of the journey of following the divine call. I remember returning to Vienna the spring after we had moved to Ireland. I sat at my father's grave and meditated with the white stones we had placed there. In Revelation 2:17, it is said that those who listen will be given a white stone with a new name. The new name is an indication that we have left behind old patterns that bind us. I am still uncertain about my new name, but I am listening, continuing to open myself to receive its gift.

The quickest way to learn to trust this unfolding is to take small steps of trust, witness what happens, and then find courage to continue forward in this way.

There are no established paths to follow. This way of *peregrinatio* is demanding as it pulls us away from what is safe and familiar. Moving us out of our comfort zones, this practice calls us to intentionally open ourselves to becoming strangers, to make the intentional journey into exile. But when we are in discernment, this is what is demanded of us, to reach beyond our familiar boundaries and patterns.

We think again of those ancient desert monks wandering out into the harsh and barren landscape, leaving behind the comforts and conveniences of city life, and becoming an exile to the normal ways of doing things, an exile to possessions and family. The Irish monks, while having no desert place, sought out wilderness spaces on the edge of the world. They sought this strangeness as essential to the spiritual path. It is in this strangeness that God can become even clearer to us. Walking toward what makes us uncomfortable and being in an environment where all of our old patterns and habits are called into question can free us to see in new ways.

I know for John and myself on this life pilgrimage to move overseas, we felt exhilarated by the prospect of living in foreign lands. The ongoing invitation has been to embrace the strangeness we so often feel—strangeness of language (even here in Ireland, there are a myriad of differing expressions for things), strangeness of culture and custom, strangeness of rhythms and relationship to time. Things do not move along as we would expect from our lives in the United States, and in that breaking of our expectations, we are broken open to a more expansive vision and possibility.

It is precisely in this place of absolute vulnerability that we can encounter a wider and wilder God. Exile calls us to soften our hard defenses, to acknowledge that we don't have all the answers, to seek the resources available in our new communities, and to reach out to strangers for support.

What are the ways you are being called into exile and strangeness in service of this holy wandering on the road of your heart?

The Journey of St. Columcille

St. Columcille, born in county Donegal, is also known as Columba (which means "dove" in Latin), and is one of the three patron saints of Ireland (in addition to St. Patrick and St. Brigid). His birth was foretold in his mother's dream of a youth receiving a radiant cloak that spread over Ireland and Scotland.

He came from a family of kings but at an early age was sent to a monastery, where he gave up his royalty and went on to found many monasteries across Ireland, including in Derry, Durrow, and Kells and as far west as the Burren in county Clare where there is still a holy well dedicated to him. He was also a poet and an artist who did illumination, including perhaps even some of those in the Book of Kells. St. Columcille refers to Jesus in his prayers as "my Druid."

Columcille experienced a call to leave Ireland and become an exile. He found it very painful and spent the night before his departure on what is now known as the "flagstone of loneliness." For many of the Irish monks, this call to exile was an integral part of the *peregrinatio* journey, to release all that is familiar and make oneself reliant on the hospitality of strangers, to feel your radical dependency on God.

In the year 563, he traveled with twelve other monks to cross the sea in a coracle and landed on a small island off the coast of Scotland, now known as Iona. It was here that he began his new work; Iona became a heart center for Celtic Christianity and is still thriving today as a vibrant community.

There is a beautiful story about his encounter with a crane. Birds were considered to be divine messengers in the Celtic world. The crane was said to be one of the first birds to greet the sunrise, the threshold time, connecting it with the direction of the east, and it is associated with knowledge and wisdom. As the Druidic tradition gave way to Christianity, sometimes the term "Crane Cleric" was used to indicate great wisdom in certain priests, such as St. Columcille.

One day a crane arrived at Iona after much travel and exhaustion. It landed on the shore quite exhausted and hungry. Columcille told one of his monks that the crane had come from Ireland and to nurse it back to strength and health for three days until it was well enough to return on its own again. The bird was lovingly tended as an honored guest in the great tradition of monastic hospitality.

I love this story for its many layers. The bird is a stranger seeking refuge and hospitality, given to it freely by the monks. The crane is a symbol of thresholds and wisdom, as it lives in the border spaces between land and sea. The three days it took to be restored links it to Christ and to the sacred number of three held dear by the Celtic imagination. Sometimes in our own journeys, we need to recognize when we are called to land for a while and seek solace and nourishment in a strange place.

Call upon St. Columcille as you move through the journey of your own life. Ask for guidance and wisdom where needed and the grace to surrender to holy direction.

Scripture Reflection by John Valters Paintner

Lectio Divina

> When Abram was ninety-nine years old, the LORD appeared to Abram, and said to him, "I am God Almighty; walk before me, and be blameless. And I will make my covenant between me and you, and will make you exceedingly numerous."
> —Genesis 17:1–2

Biblical Context

This passage in chapter 17 of the book of Genesis is the not the beginning of Abram and Sarai's story. Abram is first mentioned way back in chapter 11 (right after the Tower of Babel story), where his lineage is given. And chapter 12 is when Abram and Sarai are first called by God to leave the land of their birth in order to travel to Canaan, which eventually becomes known as the Promised Land or the Holy Land. God says to them, "Go from your country and your kindred and your father's house to the land that I will show you" (Gn 12:1).

In chapter 13, we learn that the flocks of Abram and his nephew Lot (who also traveled to Canaan with Abram and Sarai) have become so large that they must part company to find adequate grazing for their separate herds. The implication is that they have been in the Promised Land for some time and have become quite prosperous. This is further demonstrated in chapter 14 where Lot is kidnapped as part of a wider conflict in the region. Abram gathers an army of more than three hundred of his retainers and rescues Lot. (The "House of Abram and Sarai" is clearly not just a little nuclear family anymore.) The chapter ends with Abram sharing bread and wine with the priest Melchizedek before negotiating with another king. Abram and Sarai are never directly described as royalty (although the name Sarah can be translated as "princess" or "noblewoman"), but it does seem that they have equal status to the kings of the region at this point in the story.

It is not until chapter 15 that God and Abram formalize their covenant with a ritual sacrifice. The chapter begins with a rather old and childless Abram challenging God's assertion that he will be the father of a great nation. God reassures him and blesses Abram and Sarai.

In chapter 16, Sarai (impatient for a child of her own) suggests using her handmaiden, Hagar, as a surrogate mother. Abram's oldest son, Ishmael, is born to Hagar, and this leads to all sorts of family conflict between Abram, Sarai, and Hagar. It is also the basis for the debate over who is the rightful heir to the Promised Land: the descendants of Abram's eldest son, Ishmael, or Abraham's son by Sarah, Isaac.

All told, according to the text, it is twenty-four years before God gets around to telling Abram and Sarai to walk before God and change their names as a sign of a new beginning, a new life.

Personal Reflection

I think it is interesting and profound that God did not tell Abram and Sarai to "follow me." There is no "walk in my footsteps" or "this is the path I have laid out before you" language used here. No. God tells Abram and Sarai to "go on ahead." Is God telling them to go on ahead alone? Are they supposed to proceed without divine guidance? Is God going to be following them or planning on catching up later? One thing is clear: God is telling Abram and Sarai, who have already been sent forth from the land of their ancestors, to trailblaze.

But if they have already gone and arrived in the land that God has shown them, where are they being sent now? If it isn't an outer, physical journey, it must be an inner, spiritual journey. Their new names are a sign that they have been transformed by their travels and that a new, significant phase in their lives is about to begin.

It is also interesting to note that Abram's first response to being told to walk before God was to fall on his face. It reads like something I might do when given a big, new task: feel overwhelmed and freeze in indecision on how to proceed. Surely Abram must have thought either "Not again!" or "I thought I was already done with that!"

Just when Abram and Sarai are beginning to have their doubts about God's promise to them, they are suddenly faced with a question we've likely all felt at one point or another: "O Lord, now what?"

This chapter's passage may be just one of the many occasions in the Bible where we find slightly different versions of the same story, but something else seems to be happening here—something very important. While the biblical authors aren't always very good at specifying the passage of time, in these early chapters of the patriarchs and matriarchs we are told how old Abram and Sarai are when they leave the place of their birth (seventy-five and sixty-five, respectively) and how old they are when God gives them the new names Abraham and Sarah (ninety-nine and eighty-nine, respectively).

The length of time between these two events is significant enough for it to be spelled out. And twenty-four years is a serious length of time. It is enough time, perhaps, for one to lose focus or get off track. Enough time for one to need to begin again.

The idea of *peregrinatio* is that of a mysterious journey of unknown length or duration to an unknown location. But there is an end point. *Peregrinatio* isn't an unending journey. One knows when one is finished, when one has reached the place of his or her resurrection. And hadn't Abram and Sarai reached the Promised Land? They had actually arrived decades before this second calling.

At first, I found this passage a bit disheartening. After all the travel and hardships and sacrifices, don't Abram and Sarai deserve a reward . . . or at least a break? However, the longer I reflect on it, the more I see this new calling as the reward. Even at such an old age, they have more to look forward to. They have a new purpose and goal in life. Their journey is over, but a new adventure awaits them!

The Practice of *Peregrinatio*

One way to practice *peregrinatio* in our own lives is to "follow the thread," which for me means to listen to the synchronicities and patterns being revealed daily. When we are in discernment in our lives, and we pay attention to our dreams, as well as other moments that shimmer, we may begin to notice symbols showing up to call us forward.

In the desert and Celtic traditions, daily self-reflection and examination were considered to be vital to the spiritual path.

Abba Nisterus said that a monk ought to ask himself every night and every morning, "What have we done that is as God wills and what have we left undone of that which he does not will?"[5]

Abba Nisterus's counsel to ask these questions of discernment each night and each morning has much echo in Ignatius of Loyola's prayer of Examen, where we ask every day what has been most life-giving and life-draining.

This kind of daily tending of our own inner impulses and aliveness is essential for this journey of allowing ourselves to be gently guided, led sometimes from behind, lured sometimes ahead by a shimmering thread.

Consider a practice at the end of each day (or first thing in the morning if you prefer) for the coming week. In reflecting on the previous day, where have been the signs of the divine presence? Where have you felt the nudges to move forward? Where have you seen the threads calling to you? And where have you turned away from these? In what ways did you resist or ignore the holy impulses?

Photography Exploration: *Peregrinatio*

I invite you again to a contemplative walk with your camera in hand. Allow some time before you embark on the journey to center yourself through breathing and resting into the theme for this chapter.

Then let this walk be an experience of *peregrinatio* as you move through the world. Play with the experience of both looking for signs to lead you forward and also resting in the image of "walk before me"; see if you can experience the guidance of the Spirit from behind like a wind or current. Just notice what each of these experiences reveals to you. Pay attention to the world as it offers itself to you as wisdom for this call to journeying without destination. Let creation guide you to the next place.

As you move through the time, pay attention to images "shimmering" or calling out for attention. Pause and give yourself over to this object for a few minutes. Let your camera be a window into deeper seeing. If you notice yourself grasping at images, put the camera away and practice just holding a soft and loving gaze.

When you return home, look through your images and let three or four draw you to more in-depth attention. Begin by writing from the voice of the image, using the words "I am" to speak from the voice of colors, symbols, objects, shapes, and so forth, as a way of entering into this perspective on the world. Gift yourself enough time to really deepen into the experience of how these images invite you to see things.

Then shift your attention to connections between the images. As you look at all of the images in a sequence, what story do your photos want to tell? How does this telling, and allowing the words to unfold as needed, become its own form of *peregrinatio*, rather than planning it out in advance?

Writing Exploration: Seven-Line Poem

For this chapter's poem-writing exploration, I am going to suggest the form of a seven-line poem. To begin, read through your journaling from your photos (or any recent journaling you have done). As you read, circle or underline seven words that shimmer or strike you in some way or words you feel curious about exploring further.

Once you have chosen the seven, write each one on a separate slip of paper, put them all into a bag or bowl, and shuffle them.

Open your journal again, to a fresh page, and choose one slip of paper. Whichever word is on this slip, use it in the first line of your poem.

Try not to think too much about this process. Allow yourself just a minute or so to write. Also resist the temptation to choose a different word if the one that arrived isn't the one you wanted or is difficult to work into a line of poetry. Do the best you can, being gentle with yourself. Experiment and be curious and playful with the process.

Then choose a second slip of paper, and incorporate this word into the second line of your poem. Continue this way through all seven words and write seven lines of poetry inspired by each word.

This is an exercise in following the thread and where it takes you, as you do not know which word will arrive next.

Closing Blessing

We have been exploring what it means for us to wander in response to a call and seek the place of our own resurrection. I shared previously that Columcille felt some loneliness at leaving his beloved Ireland. The call brings excitement and discovery but also requires letting go and leaving behind. There is a legend that on the night before he left for his journey, he slept on what is known as the "Flagstone of Loneliness," a stone that was supposed to relieve grief. I share a poem below that I wrote about this stone.

Do you have longings to wander for love? For a deep and wise voice summoning you to the edges of your own places of comfort?

What does it feel like to yield your expectations, your sense of control, your need to figure it all out, to something greater?

flagstone of loneliness

On nights when my heart is
thick with sadness and my
limbs and sighs are ballast,
I long to lie down on the

flagstone of loneliness
like Columcille before
he sailed to Iona, leaving behind
the land he loved.

What do the stones feel as
they gather our heaviness
into their granite endurance,
so patient as clouds release
their burden of rain upon them?
Even rivers part ways for boulders,
not willing to risk splitting them wide
and unleash the channel of ancient grief.

We climb rocky summits,
under the illusion we can defy
the gravity of sorrow,
hearts pounding in exhilaration
while mountains grow weightier
under tender feet.

If you sit by a stream and listen
as water makes music over rocks,
you will hear them keening.[6]

chapter 4

The practice of blessing each moment

Deep peace of the running wave to you
Deep peace of the flowing air to you
Deep peace of the quiet earth to you
Deep peace of the shining stars to you
Deep peace of the Son of peace to you.
> —Traditional Irish Blessing

In the Celtic tradition, one of the practices that can help us with loving attention to daily life is blessing. Everything the Celts did was carried out with a reverence and sense of blessing. Blessing is really acknowledging the gifts and graces already present and entering into partnership with the divine. All the mundane activities of the day become opportunities to witness grace at work. Blessing is a way of life, and prayers are written to honor the sacred rhythms of the earth and to celebrate the ordinary tasks of the day.

Blessing is to live life from a place of gratitude, to offer thanks and honor for everything that we have, taking nothing for granted. When we remember to bless the turning of the hours and all that we do, we begin to live from an enlarged sense of being. Esther de Waal writes about "each successive task performed seriously, carefully, with attention, and simultaneously becoming the occasion for finding the presence of God, and in particular the three members of the

Trinity, since much of the work was routine and it could, therefore, be done rhythmically in the name of Father, Son, and Holy Spirit."[1] There is a meditative quality to this way of blessing as well, cultivating a habit of remembering the sacred in all things.

Blessing and Discernment

At the heart of this practice and way of life is paying mindful attention to our lives. I know hours, days, and weeks can go by sometimes before I discover I have been skimming the surface of things, preoccupied by too many tasks to complete. My calendar and to-do lists become misplaced holy grails.

All it takes is a few minutes spent pausing, being, and reflecting to rekindle my devotion to this moment. Life suddenly offers itself up as a wide expanse. We touch eternity when we bring ourselves fully here, rather than stay distracted by the rush of life's endless demands, which only serve to make us feel inadequate and always fleeting, forever anxious about too little time.

The desert mothers and fathers fled out to the deserts of Egypt and Syria in search of a place that could support their exquisite desire for unending attention to each moment as it unfolded. They knew that the soul thrives in slowness and that the divine spark of life reveals itself when we simply pay attention. The Irish monks followed them in this path as well, cultivating what was called watchfulness. It refers to a kind of calm vigilance in daily life, staying attentive to and aware of the inner movements of the heart, watching one's thoughts and noticing the patterns that arise. This inner attention, conducted with compassion, is the grace of the desert and Celtic way. When we pay attention, we remember to bless; we remember the gifts given.

The "cell" is both physical and metaphorical reality. The monks had literal cells, often caves or other simple dwellings where they could stay present and attentive. But this is also a symbolic reality, representative of the "cave of the heart" or the "inner cell," which is an interior disposition toward life. When we skate through life's endless demands on us, we lose our connection to this deep well of nourishment.

St. Benedict says in the Prologue to his Rule, "Let us then at last arouse ourselves, even as Scripture incites us in the words, 'Now is the hour for us to rise from sleep.' Let us, then, open our eyes to the divine light, and hear with our ears the divine voice as it cries out to us daily. 'Today if you hear his voice, do not harden your hearts,' and again, 'He who has ears to hear, let him hear what the Spirit says to the Churches.'"[2] The image of awakening calls us to shake off the slumber that creates a veil between reality and our perception. *Now* is the hour to awaken and arise.

Writer Jon Kabat-Zinn describes mindfulness as a kind of affectionate attention and awareness. I love that use of the word "affectionate" because it calls forth a deep sense of loving witness and compassion for ourselves. We don't attend to our unfolding experience to berate ourselves when we stray but instead to cherish the sweetness of the moments we do give our attention to. When difficult thoughts arise, we can offer loving grace to them, welcome them in, and also watch them subside again. We begin to learn the inner landscape of our own minds in this way.

The more we cultivate this kind of awareness of our thoughts, emotions, and impulses, the more we learn that they come and go, they rise and fall in intensity. Beneath all the tumultuousness of our inner lives is a profound and deep pool of stillness from which we can behold this inner drama yet not get lured into reacting to it. We develop an inner freedom and begin to discover something of the foundation of who we are, which endures no matter the constantly shifting tides around us.

This is immensely helpful when we are in the midst of discernment. We find we can begin to make decisions from a place of calm and centered grace rather than anxiety and a desire to control. Mindful attention helps us to be present to life as it actually is, rather than how we would like it to be. Blessing helps us to remember what we already have and what is good in our lives. We spend much of our lives grasping at fantasies and false securities. Bringing our full compassionate awareness to this moment invites us to receive the gift this moment has to offer. What would it mean to offer devotion to life as it really is?

Signs and Rainbows

The scripture text John will explore reveals a rainbow as a sign of the covenant. On Christmas Eve in 2014, John and I drove out to one of our local dog rescue shelters. They had issued an urgent plea for people to foster their dogs for two weeks over the holidays as all of the dog pounds close then, so they needed to make room for new dogs coming in.

We drove out on one of those days that alternated between glorious sunshine and brooding rain showers. It was perfect rainbow weather, and we saw so many that I actually lost count. All of this felt very much like a sign as we went to pick out a dog to foster for the holidays. As a friend said to me when I told her of the rainbows the next day, "This would make a great origin story."

We had been longing for a dog again, so we relished the opportunity to help the shelter out while also soaking in some canine love. We brought home Ginger Nut, an older terrier, sweet and snuggly as can be. She was a perfect companion over the Christmas season. But much to my surprise, over that time with her we actually discerned it wasn't the right season for us to have a dog in our lives. With much traveling to do, wonderful groups to be present with, and our apartment not being very well set up to take a dog out, especially for middle-of-the-night needs, we realized having a dog was not a wise choice then.

I was quite heartbroken to come to this realization, especially since Ginger Nut had worked her way into my heart. I sent the rescue folks some much better and more flattering photos of her to post in the hopes of finding her a perfect forever home. Someone saw those photos posted on Facebook and knew to whom she belonged. With all my prayers for her to find a loving place to land, what happened was even better than I had imagined. She was reunited with her guardians and went home again (and it turns out her name was Benji and she was thirteen, although she will always be Ginger Nut to me).

I felt truly overjoyed by this turn of events and grateful that I had honored the truth of my own discernment, as much as I didn't want it to be true. Ginger Nut was never meant to be ours; she was a passing guest along the way to whom we could offer some hospitality. And in return she broke my heart open in new ways; she reminded me just how much love I have to offer. She prompted a regular blessing of gratitude from my heart. The word "visitation" kept rising up for me when I considered her presence with us during that most holy of seasons. She came, offered her blessing to us, and then returned home again.

This is what happens when we start to pay attention to our lives and do the hard work of listening and responding. When we offer blessings freely as a response of gratitude to what life brings, our perspective shifts. In the Benedictine tradition, one of the central vows is obedience. On one level it means obedience to an abbot or abbess, but on a deeper level it means to follow the call of your heart, no matter how demanding or difficult. I am truly grateful for friends who supported my tender heart in the couple of days when I had to let go of the dream of having a dog and before I knew how things would unfold. Having a community of supporters, who can help us honor our discernment and who know us well enough to be able to see if the call rings true to what they know of us, is incredibly vital on this way. Signs call for blessings, the kind of spontaneous recognition from the heart.

All the dogs I have had the privilege of caring for, whether for two weeks or nine years, have been anam caras for me, "soul friends" in the Irish language; soul friendship is a practice we will be exploring in chapter 5. Ginger Nut reminded me of my own deep need to make this an even more intentional part of my life. At some point again in the future, we will be able to welcome in another canine companion. But now is not the season.

We often hold so tightly to how we want things to be that we miss what is actually being offered. The greatest grace of this experience was the affirmation that I was paying close attention. I was startled by the realization that having a dog was not the best choice for us or the dog. But I have learned to trust my intuition and to know that while resistance does have its place, we often have an inner voice we can listen for. This voice helps us to receive the gift of life as it actually is, rather than how we imagine it to be, and to bless everything that arrives.

The Journey of St. Gobnait

I only learned about St. Gobnait after moving to Ireland, but she is perhaps one of my favorite of the Irish saints. She is a fifth- and sixth-century monk who fled her home in county Clare and headed first for the island of Inisheer. It is not clear why she fled, only that she was seeking refuge on the Aran Islands. There is a beautiful church ruin there on the island still dedicated to her.

As we explored in the previous chapter, there is a deep and rich tradition among the Irish monks to seek out the place of one's resurrection by setting sail without oar or rudder to let the currents of love carry them.

The story tells us that an angel appeared to Gobnait in a dream to instruct her to go on a journey to the place where nine white deer were grazing. Only there would she find her true place of resurrection. She wandered through Waterford, Cork, and Kerry in search.

Finally, when she arrived to Ballyvourney, where there was a small rise overlooking the river Sullane, Gobnait saw nine white deer grazing all together just as the angel had promised, so she settled there and founded her monastic community.

St. Gobnait is the patron saint of bees, and there are several stories that recall her forcing invaders out of Ballyvourney by setting swarms of bees upon them. She is also the patron of the sick, and it is likely that she used honey as a healing medicine, which is considered to be one of the three great Celtic healers (the other two being water and labor).

I love this as a story of a woman who was willing to follow the invitation and recognize that what she thought was the place she was called to was in fact just a resting place along the way. In most of these stories of the saints, we have to enter in with our imagination and flesh out the human drama. Imagine being called forth to one place, settling there, and then being told in a dream to wander until the sign had been fulfilled.

I imagine her wandering the Irish landscape, searching for the white deer, and upon seeing three, and then six, her heart swelling, but continuing on until the right moment, offering blessings along the way. She paid attention to life as it unfolded. She said yes to the invitations being offered to her. She bowed down in gratitude and blessing as her call was slowly revealed.

Call upon St. Gobnait in the days ahead to help you remember to bless each activity and each day's unfolding.

Scripture Reflection by John Valters Paintner

Lectio Divina

> God said, "This is the sign of the covenant that I make between me and you and every living creature that is with you, for all future generations: I have set my bow in the clouds, and it shall be a sign of the covenant between me and the earth. When I bring clouds over the earth and the bow is seen in the clouds, I will remember my covenant that is between me and you and every living creature of all flesh; and the waters shall never again become a flood to destroy all flesh."
>
> —Genesis 9:12–15

Biblical Context

Even before the recent blockbuster film about Noah and the flood, this biblical tale is one of the more misunderstood of them all . . . at least in terms of what people think they know about it and what's actually written in the Bible. It's a story many of us grew up with. It's a favorite in illustrated children's Bibles and Sunday school classes. Then there are all the toy boats and paired animals, Noah's-ark-themed clothing and bedding, and more. Most people think they know the details, but it's my experience that not many have actually read, let alone studied, all five chapters (Genesis 5–9). Some people know that Noah was 600 years old when the flood started, but did you know that Noah sent out a crow, which did not return, before he sent the infamous dove? Or that Noah and his family brought one pair of each "unclean" animal, but seven pairs of each "clean" animal? (The people were vegetarian before the flood and only allowed to eat the "clean" animals after the flood, as it would take a while for all the drowned vegetation to regrow.) And how many, particularly those who wrote letters to the movie studio demanding that the Russell Crowe film be "biblically accurate," know that the story ends with Noah getting drunk and naked?

However, beyond the details of the story there is the larger context. In the creation stories, God creates order out of chaos. In the first creation story, God separates the waters and makes a pocket of dry land and air between the heavens above and the heavens below, in which all living things are placed (a reverse snow globe, if you will, with the water on the outside). God creates everything in an orderly and purposeful manner. Only once all is prepared are man and woman created. God looked on all that had been created and declared it "good." In the second creation story, Adam and Eve sin. They are kicked out of the Garden of Eden and face hardship, including aging and death. Unfortunately, sin continues to spread: jealousy and arrogance lead to murder and the destruction of society. As sin grows, so do the consequences. Each generation is consecutively shorter lived; eventually God decides to start over with Noah and his family, who find blessing from God and are chosen to save enough of creation to start it over again.

Personal Reflection

When we first moved to Austria in 2012, I expected life to be very different. I knew the language was different. I knew enough to realize the culture was going to be different from anything I'd ever experienced before. I expected the unexpected and was delighted to discover it. However, having grown up in a largely Irish-American family and a parish filled with Irish immigrant priests and nuns, when we then moved to Ireland I expected life to feel much more familiar.

I was wrong.

Living in Austria was like living on a different planet. Living in Ireland has been more akin to living in a parallel universe. Most things are the same and recognizable, but every time I think I've got things figured out . . . I realize I do not. It's been a continuing lesson in patience and humility, in the best possible sense.

One of my greatest frustrations with life in Ireland (as much as I truly love it here) is the sporadic nature of street and road signs. The ones that are there are adequate but not great. It is when the signs just aren't there that I feel the road rage grow. I often think it would be easier, or at least easier to accept, if there were no signs at all. Then I would not get my hopes up. I think I could learn to deal without them, as there would be no other choice.

I know this is my American bias coming into play. I expect things to be as they always were, or at least as they were when I grew up. I take it for granted that every street across the nation, whether it be in the middle of a major city or out in the country, will be labeled in the same manner. I want so much for things to be the way I like them or am used to them that I am caught unaware almost every time things are different.

Consistency is what I crave. The lesson for me here is to be more appreciative of the signs that are there, whether they are from the Irish transportation ministry or God. Life, like driving in Ireland, would be so much easier with more signs and a lot more difficult without any. And like driving in Ireland, I long for more assurance from God. But can I truly say I do not have enough? Isn't it my unrealistic expectations (and grumbling) that cause me more problems?

How ungrateful is it for me to whine about not being blessed enough?

Like so many who think they know Noah's story, what I lack is a mindful attention to what's actually there (rather than my obsessive focus on what I think should be there). Instead of anger over unfulfilled expectations, I should be more appreciative of the many blessings I do have, like my driving navigator and anam cara, Christine.

I take a small comfort in knowing that I am not alone in sometimes being oblivious to what's right in front of me because I am too caught up in what I want to be there. We humans can often be very good at self-delusion. I get the concept behind the phrase "Fake it 'til you make it," but it helps to be self-aware enough to know that one is faking it. When we believe our own hype and propaganda, we miss out on a great deal in life.

I am often struck, in the prophetic texts of the Hebrew Scriptures, by the prophets' ability to see the difference between what is and what should be. Sometimes I get so caught up in the "what should be" part, that I miss out on the "what is" aspect of life. I sometimes complain so much about the rain that I miss the rainbow.

The blessings of life are there to be seen by those willing to look.

Br. David Steindl-Rast, O.S.B., (a spiritual guide whose teachings have been very important and inspirational to Christine and me) preaches about gratefulness. It can only be achieved when we are paying attention to what is before us. And it is only in genuinely seeing what is before us that we can have true appreciation and love for the ways we have been blessed.

Br. David was a young Austrian teenager during World War II. He witnessed much destruction and death. He never expected to survive the war. And so when he did, he was faced with a choice: to continue to live in fear of death or to see each moment of life as a blessing to be seized and appreciated. We, too, have that same choice each moment. Will we miss the blessings or will we see, and be, the blessing?

The Practice of Blessing Each Moment

One of the beautiful practices of the Celtic tradition is blessing the world, blessing each and every encounter and experience, the most ordinary moment. I am reminded as well of the beautiful Jewish practice of blessing all the elements of our days. In these worldviews, each act becomes worthy of blessing. Gratitude is offered for the gift of every moment—when waking, crossing a threshold, eating a meal, lighting candles. The Talmud calls for one hundred blessings each day. This act of blessing is really a special way of paying attention. It is mindfulness infused with gratitude. It is a moment of remembering wonder as our primary response to the world. It is an act of consecrating time.

In the Benedictine monastic tradition, everything is considered sacred. The stranger at the door is to be welcomed in as Christ. The kitchen utensils are to be treated just like the altar vessels. The hinges of the day call us to remember the presence of God again and again, so that time becomes a cascade of prayers.

So what if I imagine my eyes as a vessel of blessing? What if I move through the day, and each time I begin a new task, I pause and consecrate what I am about to do?

Perhaps I might even say a short prayer: "Bless this shimmering moment; may my eyes receive its gifts; may my heart open ever wider in response." You might craft your own unique holy words.

We can begin to see all the everyday details of our lives as openings into the depth dimension of the world. The steam rising from my coffee, the bird singing from a tree branch outside my window, the doorbell announcing a friend's arrival, the meal that nourishes my body for service. Each of these moments invites us to pause and to see it through a different kind of vision.

Esther de Waal describes the daily rhythm of Celtic monks as one of reverence and attentiveness to the tools they worked with, each activity of the day done in partnership with God. This blessing of the kitchen is attributed to St. Brigid:

Oh, my Prince
Who canst do all these things,
Bless O God—a cry unforbidden—
My kitchen with Thy right hand!
My kitchen.
The kitchen of the white God,
A kitchen which my King hath blessed,
A kitchen that hath butter.
Mary's Son, my Friend cometh
To bless my kitchen[3]

The kitchen is a holy place, the office is a sanctuary, the bedroom is a place of divine rest and revelation, the world at our feet shimmers brightly each moment if we only have eyes to see. God is with me moment by moment, and blessings remind me of this truth.

Photography Exploration: Mindful Attention

I invite you to once again go on a contemplative walk with the frame of "mindful attention" as your intention for your time out gazing on the world.

As you walk, stay connected to your breath and simply stay aware of what is unfolding moment by moment. Bring loving compassion to your experience. Stay present to any "signs" that may arrive, remembering that they may be subtle. Just notice what shimmers for you in the world or stirs your heart, and receive it. As you walk, bless everything you see and notice how that shifts your relationship to it.

When you return home, allow some time to be with the images that arrived. Let one or two of them choose you as symbolic of your experience and write about the process of receiving them. Pay special attention to any that felt like they might be "signs" speaking to you.

Then spend time with each one and speak from its voice, using the words "I am." Write from the perspective of this image. For example, if you received an image of the sea, you might write, "I am the sea. I move with the rhythms of the moon; I am fierce and relenting; I am gentle and womblike." This is just an example; when you enter into the voice of the image, really imagine seeing the world from this perspective.

If your photo has multiple images, you can speak from each one. For example, in my photo of the sea, I might also speak with the voice of the sky, the wave, a seagull, a shell, and so forth. Let yourself really explore all of the possibilities in the image.

Writing Exploration: Blessings for Daily Life

Your invitation is to carry the spirit of blessing to everything you do. Blessing is a way of holding a heart of gratitude for the multitude of gifts we experience moment by moment. What would it be like to pause before each activity and encounter and bless the time and experience? Blessing means to make holy, but in this context, I think what we are really doing is honoring the holiness already present. We are naming God at work already within and around us.

Consider writing a blessing for the creatures in your life, whether domesticated animals or wild ones you encounter out in nature. Bless the unfolding rhythms of the day and the cathedrals of creation that inspire you. Bless the food you eat as nourishment from the earth to sustain your life and service.

Closing Blessing

I offer you a poem I wrote about St. Gobnait, inspired by her journey to find the place of her resurrection—which demanded that she pay attention, bless the way as she went, and consecrate her arrival.

What are the challenges for you of mindful attention? What are the signs shimmering out to you that you want to keep paying attention to?

st. gobnait and the place of her resurrection

On the tiny limestone island
an angel buzzes to Gobnait
in a dream, disrupts her plans,
sends her in search of nine white deer.

She wanders for miles across
sea and land until at last
they appear and rather than
running toward them

she falls gently to wet ground,
sits in silence as light crawls across sky,
lets their long legs approach
and their soft, curious noses surround her.

Breathing slowly, she slides back
onto grass and clover and knows
nothing surpasses this moment,
a heaven of hooves and dew.

Is there a place for each of us,
where we no longer yearn to be elsewhere?
Where our work is to simply soften,
wait, and pay close attention?

She smiles as bees gather eagerly
around her too, wings humming softly
as they collect essence of wildflowers,
transmuting labor into gold.[4]

chapter 5

The practice of soul friendship

Another key practice of both desert and Celtic saints was having a soul friend, an *anam cara*. The desert elders were sought out by thousands desiring a deeper life of faith, seeking wisdom that comes from life experience. Patrick and Brigid both expressed how vital this was for their lives. St. Brigid is often quoted as saying, "Go forth and eat nothing until you get a soul-friend, for anyone without a soul-friend is like a body without a head; is like the water of a polluted lake, neither good for drinking nor for washing. That is the person without a soul-friend."[1]

Everyone, whether lay or clergy, man or woman, was expected to have a spiritual mentor and companion on the soul's journey. This was a person to whom you could confide all of the inner struggles, someone who would help you find your path and could midwife you in discernment. There was a sense of genuine warmth and intimacy in this relationship and a deep respect for the other's wisdom as a source of blessing. Age or gender differences did not matter.

Irish priest John O'Donohue writes, "The anam ċara was a person to whom you could reveal the hidden intimacies of your life. This friendship was an act of recognition and belonging. When you had an anam ċara, your friendship cut across all convention and category. You were joined in an ancient and eternal way with the friend of your soul."[2]

The same holds true today. There should not be wandering from one soul friend to another or else there is the danger of only a superficial relationship. Full honesty and truthfulness are expected. The tradition of having a soul friend reinforces the communal and corporate nature of Celtic spirituality and the dangers of traveling the spiritual path alone.

A soul friend offers us the courage needed to say yes to the big dreams being birthed in us. They help us to gain clarity over places of self-deception and denial. It is said that Patrick used to have an angel named Victor who visited him regularly and offered Patrick his guidance, sometimes in dreams. Victor was a kind of guardian spirit. Soul friends can be those who have passed through the veil and continue to offer us support and wisdom.

On a journey of discernment, perhaps our greatest ally is a wise mentor who has been through the journey already. It is painful to experience exile, but if we can find someone who can reassure us—because of his or her own experience—that this journey is essential to our own authenticity, we can find solace and endurance.

Esther de Waal, in her book *The Celtic Way of Prayer: The Recovery of the Religious Imagination,* writes, "The relationship of soul-friendship existed between men and women, women and women, men and men, cleric and lay. The soul-friend was the spiritual guide who helped everyone to find his or her own path. The practice of seeing one's soul-friend on a regular basis seems to have been expected by all who committed themselves to the relationship."[3]

I invite you to seek out a soul friend. You may already have one in your life, a spiritual director, a wise guide, someone you can turn to when things feel challenging and "entrust the secrets of your heart." A soul friend acts as a witness, someone who affirms where we are and can offer counsel when we want to run far away. This is why the spiritual journey is always done in community.

If having a spiritual director is not feasible, consider if there is someone in your life with whom you could have an intentional conversation about the soul's journey, someone who knows you well and can help illuminate your blind spots.

Discernment and the Inner Multitude

We each contain within ourselves a multitude of energies and desires, often conflicting with one another. We are spontaneous, soulful, scandalous; we are son or daughter, worker, lover, obedient one, rebel, friend, enemy, planner, wise woman or man, inner child, and much more.

Jungian psychologist Chelsea Wakefield has a helpful book called *Negotiating the Inner Peace Treaty* in which she explores how to work with these inner selves. In the process of learning to honor each of these sub-personalities, we are able to strengthen our inner Witness, that aspect of ourselves able to behold each aspect from a calm and compassionate place, allowing each to have voice.

Often what happens in our discernment process is that we have a whole host of competing inner voices that each have an opinion about which way to go next, creating anxiety and sometimes paralysis.

What also happens is that we over-identify with one or more identities. For example, if we are very invested in being pastors or spiritual directors, we may find great value and confidence in being seen as wise and compassionate, as being the ones others turn to in times of crisis or struggle. But if this is the sole source of our identities, we may also find ourselves feeling confined. We have to make sure we always "look the part," and anytime we begin to struggle or have doubts, it becomes quite painful because our façades are cracking.

This can be profoundly important in our discernment as we listen to the longings held by the different parts of ourselves. Maybe one part desires a strong sense of security and being rooted at home, while another longs to set off to distant horizons and cast off the need for certainties. We are called to make room for all of the voices. This is where a soul friend can be essential, in helping us to see the old personas and masks we wear that can be released and to honor and name the gifts we bring, which have gone unnoticed and unnamed.

Soul friends play an essential role in helping us to welcome in the inner stranger. Often meeting these parts of ourselves that have been abandoned again and again brings on tears of recognition and homecoming.

The Grace of Tears

When I contemplate my sins, grant me tears always,
for great are the claims of tears on cheeks.
Grant me tears when rising, grant me tears when
  resting,
beyond your every gift altogether for love of you,
Mary's Son. Grant me tears in bed to moisten my
  pillow,
so that his dear ones may help to cure the soul.
—Excerpt from Irish poem

In the desert tradition, the *ammas* and *abbas* wrote often about the gift that tears bring. We are called to be fully present to the full spectrum of our experiences. The hermit in her or his cell carries all the wounds and pain into the cave of the heart. The Celtic monks, deeply inspired by the desert tradition, also embraced tears as essential to the spiritual path. Other Celtic poems ask God for "fierce floods of tears" or describe the "baptism of tears." St. Columcille, who left Ireland to found Iona in Scotland, wrote in his rule for his community to "pray until the tears come."

The Celtic imagination is aware of the brokenness of the human heart. The Irish high crosses often feature an image of Adam and Eve sharing the apple in the Garden of Eden while also showing St. Anthony and St. Paul sharing a loaf of bread in the Egyptian desert, holding the stories of fallenness and reconciliation together. Anthony and Paul were certainly soul friends, holding each other accountable on the spiritual way.

In monasticism, holy tears are the tears of compunction. When we are discerning, often tears arise over paths not taken in the past or possibilities unavailable to us in the future. These are tears of loss and bereavement, of discovering that we have been concealing our gifts under the expectations of others, of grieving over lost time and wasted opportunities to become closer to God. These are the tears that lead us to conversion, to a deep change of heart, another monastic principle. The root of "compunction" is the Latin word *punctio*, which means "a puncture" or "pricking pain." Compunction describes the experience of having our hearts pierced by sorrow and made soft and fleshy once again.

When we have a soul friend, we have someone with whom we can share these moments of tenderness with. They need to be witnessed and held in loving intimacy.

How might I welcome in the gift of tears? What are the losses that have gone unmourned because of the busyness of my life or my unwillingness to sit with the darkness?

This gift of tears reveals to us the perfectionism, the games, the manipulations, and the stories we tell ourselves. They free us from lying and any form of pretense that takes over when we feel anxious.

Tears of compunction (*penthos*, in Greek) arise when we are awakened to realities that had been, until now, hidden beneath our conscious awareness. Often they are stirred when we deepen our contemplative practice and begin to get in touch with all the ways we have turned away from God and from ourselves. We discover something authentic and meaningful, and grief is unleashed over having ignored it for so long. Tears often emerge when the moment is ripe for us to see in a new way. Tears also arise when we recognize the ways we have been forcing the ripening within us, rather than allowing it to happen.

You have likely had the experience where you were sitting in silence and suddenly a great sadness rose up in you and you weren't certain where it came from. Prayer works through the many layers of our defenses so that we keep discovering what feel like new levels of grief and sorrow at how far away we have allowed ourselves to wander from the heart.

Alan Jones describes saints as those who "have been allowed to see into themselves and have not refused to look."[4] This reminds me of David Whyte's provocative question in one of his poems: "Why are we the one terrible part of creation privileged to refuse our own flowering?"[5] The path of brokenness is lined with all the ways we have refused to look at our wounds and all the moments we have refused our own flowering.

In discerning the authenticity of the gift, the desert and Celtic monks invite us to ask whether our weeping draws us closer to others and creation. They call us to consider whether our own capacity to weep with others who weep is expanded. These tears are in service to our own growing compassion, both for ourselves and for the world.

St. Kevin and the Blackbird

The story of St. Kevin and the Blackbird is another one of my favorite stories about Celtic saints. He was a sixth-century monk and abbot who was a soul friend to many, including Ciaran of Clonmacnoise. After he was ordained, he retreated to a place of solitude, most likely near the Upper Lake at Glendalough, where there is a place called "St. Kevin's bed."

He lived there as a hermit for seven years, sleeping on stone and eating very simply: only nuts, herbs, and water. In the writings of his life, it is said that all of creation would sing to him. Kevin is known for his intimacy with nature and animals. It is said that when he was an infant and a young child, a white cow used to come to offer him milk. Later, after he founded his community, an otter would bring salmon from the lake for him to eat.

One of the most well-known stories about him tells that he would pray every day in a small hut, with arms outstretched. The hut was so small, though, that one arm reached out the window. One day, a blackbird landed in his palm and slowly built a nest there. Kevin realized what was happening and knew that he could not pull his hand back with this new life being hatched in it. So he spent however many days it took for the eggs to be laid, the tiny birds to hatch, and the fledglings to ready themselves to fly away with his hand outstretched.

I love this story because it evokes such an image of yielding, of surrendering to something that was "not in the plans" and receiving it as gift. Instead of sitting there in agony trying to figure out how to move the bird, he enters into this moment with great love and hospitality.

How many times in our lives do we reach out our hands for a particular purpose, and something else arrives? It is something that may cause discomfort, something we may want to pull away from, but in our wiser moments we know that this is a holy gift we are invited to receive.

There are stories of St. Columbanus, during his periods of fasting and prayer in places of solitude, calling the creatures to himself, and they running eagerly toward him. Esther de Waal says, "He would summon a squirrel from the tree tops and let it climb all over him, and from time to time its head might be seen peeping through the folds of his robes."[6] Animals such as bears and wolves, normally feared and hunted, were shown warmth and kindness and responded with mutual respect.

Celtic tradition is full of legends about kinship and intimacy between monks and the wild animals of the forests where they lived. Sometimes the creatures were the ones to lead hermits to their places of prayer and solitude. De Waal tells of St. Brynach, who had a dream in which an angel told him to go along the bank of the river until he saw "a wild white sow with white piglings,"[7] and they would show him the spot for his hermitage. Often the animal that would show the monk his or her cell would stay on as a companion, the two sharing life together.

This is our call in soul friendship as well, to learn how to yield our own agendas and egos and allow ourselves to be vulnerable and transparent in front of another. To show our shadow and tender places, to seek growth knowing that what is kept hidden only festers. When speaking with a soul friend, keep in mind this open-palmed approach to life, not needing to hold too tightly to your own façade or the persona you present in life.

Call upon St. Kevin to help you to find a soul friend, someone with whom you can show your most vulnerable self.

Scripture Reflection by John Valters Paintner

Lectio Divina

> Ruth said,
> "Do not press me to leave you
>   or to turn back from following you!
> Where you go, I will go;
>   where you lodge, I will lodge;
> your people shall be my people,
>   and your God my God.
> Where you die, I will die—
>   there will I be buried.
> May the Lord do thus and so to me,
>   and more as well,
> if even death parts me from you!"
> When Naomi saw that she was determined to go with
>   her, she said no more to her.
>   —Ruth 1:16–18

Biblical Context

There is much that is xenophobic in the Hebrew Scriptures. Gentiles are scapegoated in numerous passages as the source of temptation. There are commandments and warnings from the prophets to stay away from outsiders as a means to help the Chosen People keep the covenant. They are told to only marry their children off to families from the twelve tribes of Israel. Then there are other nations of people, such as the loosely related Moabite tribe across the Jordan River, that are specifically barred by name from intermarriage.

Most stories in the book of Judges are tales of religious warriors being called forth to defeat the Israelite's oppressors and return the people to the covenant. It is in this era of military and religious oppression that the book of Ruth is set. And it is about a gentile, a

Moabite no less, who proves to be more loyal to God and the covenant than any Israelite.

Her tale began when a couple from Bethlehem, Elimelech and Naomi, took their two sons Mahlon and Chilion to the plateau of Moab because of a famine in the Promised Land. Elimelech died shortly after arriving, but Naomi stayed and her sons married Moabite women, Ruth and Orpah. Ten years passed, and Naomi's sons also died before either of them had children of their own.

A childless widow, Naomi decided to return to her homeland now that the famine was over and she had nothing left in Moab. At first, her daughters-in-law went with her, but Naomi convinced Orpah to return to her family in the hope that they would be able to find her a new husband so she might have a family of her own. Ruth, however, refused to leave Naomi and uttered the words I began this reflection with in what I consider one of the most powerful statements of love and loyalty in the entire Bible.

Naomi returned to Bethlehem, and Ruth, knowing this would be her fate, gleaned for scraps to feed herself and her mother-in-law. When Ruth was fortunate enough to glean in the field of a pious relative of Elimelech, Naomi hatched a scheme.

What happens next is vaguely written and can be interpreted two different ways. The traditional interpretation is that Ruth symbolically presented herself as a servant to Boaz, lying at his feet as a way to say that she'd accept if he were to propose marriage. The alternative interpretation is that Ruth seduced Boaz.

Either way, the next morning Boaz dissuaded another potential rival for Ruth's hand in marriage. Boaz and Ruth married, and Naomi went to live under Boaz's roof. Ruth begot Obed. Obed begot Jesse. Jesse begot David. David begot the kingdom of Israel.

Ruth's loyalty to Naomi is rewarded with a wealthy and pious husband. Naomi's loyalty to Ruth is rewarded with a grandson. Both women are rewarded in a way that would seem to uphold the patriarchy and traditional gender roles. However, it is the very nontraditional friendship of these two women, bridging both generational and cultural differences, that is the true reward.

Personal Reflection

As a lifelong introvert, growing up I never really had a lot of close friends. Sure, I had my older sisters and cousins and classmates, but I was never one for a huge circle of mates. I was blessed with several "best friends" through the years, in grade school and college. However, they were relationships that came and went as time passed and people moved.

When I met Christine, all that changed. I know that everyone's marriage is different, but this isn't about Christine and I being spouses; it's about us being true soul friends.

We certainly don't always agree on all things (a fact with which she will, ironically, readily agree). But they are minor disagreements that we work through. At the end of the day, like Ruth and Naomi, we have followed each other to foreign lands to live out our calling. We support and sometimes challenge each other to be our best selves.

Christine didn't move from her native New York to my hometown specifically to meet me. She didn't even stay in California a year after her time as a Jesuit volunteer to be with me. We met after she had decided to stay on the West Coast a bit longer than originally planned. And we made the decision to stay in Sacramento after we married.

Our first mutually agreed move was to the Bay Area to be closer to our graduate school in Berkeley. But when we were done with our programs, we made the tough decision to leave my family and her mother (who had moved from New York City to Sacramento to be closer to us) and pursue a calling in the Pacific Northwest.

Nine years later, like Naomi and Ruth, we were once again called back to the motherland of our ancestors. In many ways it was a difficult move, as we had to leave behind our family and friends. And we had just gotten our condo and our lives to a place where we felt very comfortable.

God had other plans.

What made this move easier, what to this day assures me that it has been the right decision, is that through it all (and it hasn't all been easy), I have had my anam cara at my side. We have new work, new friends, and even a new home. But what makes it "home" is her, a soul friend who both comforts me when I am conflicted and conflicts me when I am too comfortable.

Now, as I mentioned briefly at the beginning of this reflection, soul friends are not limited to lifelong partners such as a spouse. Soul friendship is not a specifically sacramental relationship in that sense. I have had several friends I would consider soul friends, people who have come and gone from my life and acted as informal spiritual directors and mentors. I may have lost contact with these people over the years through my many travels, but the impact they had on my life is no less profound. Soul friends take many forms and can involve either a lifelong pairing or a transitory encounter. But there is always a deep sense of commitment, if only for short time, to another incarnated soul.

The Practice of Soul Friendship

I feel fortunate to have had different kinds of soul friends in my life. Certainly John, as my beloved spouse, is also the person in my life with whom I am most intimate. He knows most of my failings as well as my gifts. In countless ways, his love for me has healed many long-standing wounds from childhood. The places in our lives where we conflict are just as valuable as the places where we come together in unison. It is a gift to witness his life's unfolding alongside my own and see how they might weave together.

I also have a spiritual director who takes on that more formal role and whom I meet with regularly. As someone who does this kind of work with others, it is essential for me to have someone who can hold space for my process. He is a Jungian analyst near Seattle, Washington, and I began to see him a couple years after my mother died. I struggled deeply at that time with depression and what I later came to recognize as a dark night of the soul. My image of God was being broken apart, and he accompanied me on the slow path to embracing a wider one. When I moved overseas, I first assumed I would go on to find a new spiritual director in my new home country. But after we moved from Seattle to Vienna, everything and everyone was new and I was hungry for people in my life who already knew my story. So I was grateful to be able to continue our connection by Skype, a relationship that endures now that I live in Ireland, and I love that he has known my journey for these many years and can help illuminate patterns and reveal shadow places. He has been a wise guide in my life for more than ten years now, for which I am deeply grateful.

I also have several very dear and close women friends whom I would consider soul friends in my life. They are women with whom I share regular conversations about the goings-on of life who always reach down beneath the superficial layers and into the matters of the heart. These are women who know me well and help support me and challenge me.

I have also been blessed many times in my life with animals that have acted as soul friends. I am a dog person through and through, and I cherish how my connection to animal wisdom deepens my own path. While living in Sacramento, the Bay Area, and Seattle, our dogs were long-term members of the family. When we first adopted Tune, an eight-year-old Weimaraner who had spent her life in a breeding kennel utterly neglected, her gratitude for her new life was palpable. She bonded to us immediately, even as she continued to be wary of other people. She taught me much in her four years with us about healing the wounds of the heart, about slow rhythms, about unconditional love. Now with all the groups and travel in our lives for work, we aren't yet in a position to commit long-term to a dog, so we have fostered dogs over the last three Christmases when our schedules have been much slower. Each of those dogs—Ginger Nut, Melba, and Sisi—have revealed something to me of the holy and have asked me to stretch into deeper and wilder understandings of how the sacred is made visible.

And finally, I have also found—much like St. Patrick—that my ancestors and others who have passed through the veil can continue to act as soul friends. Certainly the witness of people such as St. Hildegard of Bingen and St. Benedict of Nursia continue to nourish and challenge my path. Time and space are not limits on this relationship. Many in Ireland would call on St. Brigid to be a daily companion and guide in the tasks of life.

Photography Exploration: Shadow and Light

I invite you again into a contemplative walk with a special focus or attention this time on the interplay of shadow and light. You have been exploring your inner and outer multitude, all those parts that you choose to welcome in, as well as those parts you would prefer to keep hidden.

Prepare by allowing some time to center yourself, breathing deeply to drop inward. Remember this is a walk of paying attention to what unfolds moment by moment. You do not need to figure out where you are going or what will happen in this time. Let it all come to you as gift.

Before you set out, bring your awareness to your heart center and ask for the grace to see with heart-centered vision and to receive whatever gifts are offered. Carry your camera with you, and for this walk, pay special attention to shadow and light. Notice the way shadows are formed, playing with the shapes of things.

When you return home, allow a couple of images to choose you and spend some time journaling with them. Speak from their voice of the symbols you find in your images as you have done in previous chapters. Make sure to allow time to speak the "I am" from the perspective of shadow figures.

After exploring at least two or three voices, bring them into dialogue with one another. What do they have to say to you and to one another?

End with a question for each: "What have you come to reveal to me about my own shadows?" Listen for what response rises up.

Writing Exploration: "I want to know . . ."

To begin your writing exploration, I invite you to read the poem "Self-Portrait" by David Whyte. Read it through slowly twice, letting the images make an impression on you.

It doesn't interest me if there is one God
or many gods.
I want to know if you belong or feel
abandoned.
If you know despair or can see it in others.
I want to know
if you are prepared to live in the world
with its harsh need
to change you. If you can look back
with firm eyes
saying this is where I stand. I want to know
if you know
how to melt into that fierce heat of living
falling toward
the center of your longing. I want to know
if you are willing
to live, day by day, with the consequence of love
and the bitter
unwanted passion of your sure defeat.

I have heard, in that fierce embrace, even
the gods speak of God.[8]

Then take his refrain of "I want to know" and do some free writing, starting each sentence with those words. What do you want to know? What are the deepest questions for you right now?

Then speak from the voice of some of your shadow images from the photography exploration. Write "I want to know" from their perspective and see where their voice takes you.

After allowing some time to write without censoring and just seeing what images come, you might craft some of these phrases into a poem. Resist the urge to edit or get things "perfect." We are going for honesty and discovery.

Closing Blessing

We have explored the gift of soul friends in our lives and how they come in many shapes and forms. Soul friends help us to navigate the inner dimensions of ourselves, the holy tears that may come on our journey, and help to hold us accountable. If you haven't had a soul friend before, I hope that you have considered how you might invite that relationship into your life. If you do have that in your life, I hope you might be experiencing even more gratitude for the ways this person blesses your unfolding journey.

I close here with a poem I wrote, inspired by the story of St. Kevin and the Blackbird. I believe strongly that animals and nature offer us windows into the spiritual life that we don't receive in other ways.

st. kevin holds open his hand

Imagine being like Kevin,
your grasping fist softens,
fingers uncurl and
palms open, rest upward,
and the blackbird
weaves twigs and straw and bits of string
in the begging bowl of your hand,
you feel the delicate weight of
speckled blue orbs descend,
and her feathered warmth
settling in for a while.

How many days can you stay,
  open,
    waiting
for the shell
to fissure and crack,
awaiting the slow emergence
of tiny gaping mouths
and slick wings
that need time to strengthen?

Are you willing to wait and watch?
To not withdraw your
affections too soon?
Can you fall in love with the
exquisite ache in your arms
knowing the hatching it holds?

Can you stay not knowing
how broad those wings will
become, or how they will fly
awkwardly at first,
then soar above you

until you have become the sky
and all that remains is
your tiny shadow
swooping across the earth?[9]

chapter 6

The practice of encircling

In the Celtic monastic tradition, a lorica is a type of prayer seeking protection, invoking the power of God to safeguard us against darker forces. The word *lorica* means "shield" and would originally have been a Druidic prayer engraved by soldiers on shields and breastplates as they went into battle. The biblical inspiration may come from Ephesians 6:14, which refers to putting on the breastplate of righteousness. The roots of this prayer may extend back to the time of the Druids, as many of these Celtic practices do.

In her book *Holy Companions: Spiritual Practices from the Celtic Saints*, Mary Earle writes that the tradition of the breastplate prayer is closely tied to St. Patrick. "A lorica prayer allows one to call on the presence of Christ, in whom 'all things hold together' (Col 1:17)."[1]

Likely the prayer is rooted in the precarious sense we often have of our own existence. Travelers would have especially faced dangers at night from thieves or wild animals, when only fire and prayer would have been their protection. People are faced with the realities of illness, war, and poverty. Every culture seems to have a sense of the conflict between powers of goodness and evil.

This fundamental struggle is an archetypal one and often at the root of our feeling divided from ourselves. We see some energies within us as bad and so suppress them, while others we value and so uplift. In our current times, there is much talk of building walls to keep out the "other," yet we forget that the "other" already dwells within us in the form of our shadows.

69

Most often the dark forces we battle with on a daily basis are within our own hearts. This was what prompted many of the desert and Celtic monks to flee to the wilderness, to have a place free of other distraction to do battle with these interior energies.

While battle may be a metaphor many of us feel uncomfortable with, we must acknowledge that this interior conflict rages on. Each of us has a shadow side that we fear to examine; we each have an ego-centered dimension that loves to live in illusion and thrives from striving and accomplishment. When we deny these parts of ourselves, they manifest in various forms such as fear, depression, addiction, despair, anxiety, and relationships built on dysfunction. We see these on a cultural scale as well.

These can be powerful prayers when we acknowledge our own places of woundedness and ask for protection from the inner struggles we all face. It becomes an unhealthy practice when we see all the evil forces as "out there" and don't claim our own shadow work. This is rooted in a profound sense of our fragility as human beings.

You are probably most familiar with the lorica prayer attributed to St. Patrick:

I arise today through the strength of heaven;
light of sun, radiance of moon,
splendor of fire, speed of lightning,
swiftness of wind, depth of the sea,
stability of earth, firmness of rock.
I arise today through God's strength to pilot me,
God's eye to look before me,
God's wisdom to guide me,
God's way to lie before me,
God's shield to protect me
from all who shall wish me ill,
afar and a-near,
alone and in a multitude,
against every cruel, merciless power
that may oppose my body and soul.
Christ with me, Christ before me,
Christ behind me, Christ in me,

Christ beneath me, Christ above me,
Christ on my right, Christ on my left,
Christ when I lie down, Christ when I sit down,
Christ when I arise, Christ to shield me,
Christ in the heart of everyone who thinks of me,
Christ in the mouth of everyone who speaks of me,
I arise today.[2]

This breastplate prayer names the presence of Christ in all directions as a shield against harm and a reminder of the divine indwelling. These kinds of encircling prayers were quite common in the Irish and Celtic tradition, and they remind the one who calls upon them that God is present everywhere.

Similarly, this lorica of St. Fursa asks that God encircle the one who is being blessed:

May the yoke of the Law of God be on this shoulder.
May the coming of the Holy Spirit be on this head.
May the sign of Christ be on this forehead.
May the hearing of the Holy Spirit be in these.[3]

This prayer, attributed to St. Fursa of the eighth century, is an act of surrender to God's faithful watch. The monk is calling upon divine boundaries and protection to be embodied in his very being.

Encircling and Discernment

Often in church communities, the word "no" is looked down upon. There can be pressure to accept invitations and requests to help as a sacrifice. Women in particular are often taught that taking care of oneself is a selfish act.

Creating strong and healthy boundaries is an essential part of this encircling prayer, and we need protection from forces that might drain us of our energy and leave us too depleted to do the work that keeps us feeling most alive. Imagine praying over your calendar and asking God to encircle you and guide you to what could be left off the schedule to give you more time.

Other times, boundaries are needed with unhealthy relationships. Perhaps we have a coworker who is toxic or a relative who is always critical, never offering anything supportive to say. Perhaps a friendship has come to an end because we are moving in different directions in our lives and we realize that we need to conserve our energy for those who truly nourish us. Consider if there are people in your life whom you could step back from or, in the case of a coworker, ask for God's assistance and protection when dealing with that person.

Even the daily news can be a source of onslaught to our sensitive energies. I think this is true now more than ever. We can easily become overwhelmed by all the terrible things happening in the world. The encircling prayer can help us to discern what is ours to respond to and what we can simply grieve.

When we are in discernment about next steps in our lives, no is as vital as yes. Knowing where we do not want to put our energy and attention is as important as where we do want to direct them.

The Call of St. Patrick

Patrick is the patron saint of Ireland and the most well-known of all the Irish saints. He was born in 390 either near England's west coast or in Wales. When he was about sixteen years old, he was captured by pirates and taken to Ireland, where he lived as a slave for six years. He endured many hardships, including hunger, thirst, and cold under the rule of a cruel pagan king.

It was during his enslavement, while spending long hours in solitude tending sheep, that he had a spiritual awakening. Through the prompting of dreams and other voices, Patrick was able to escape and return back home again. He set out for Gaul to learn theology and prepare himself for his future ministry. After many years passed, he had another dream in which he heard the Irish people calling out to him to return to the land of his enslavement.

Patrick means "one who frees hostages," and when he returned to Ireland, he was very vocal in his opposition to slavery.

He returned there in 432 and spent the rest of his life preaching the message of Christianity and helping establish the Christian

Church in Ireland. There is a great deal of evidence that Patrick was not the one to bring Christianity to Ireland, that it had already begun to flower, but certainly he was instrumental in its continued growth.

I find his story intriguing. Here was a man enslaved, who escaped by divine intervention, and then heard the call to return to the land of his slavery—and he went willingly. He must have experienced more than his share of discomfort at the thought.

There are churches founded by Patrick in the area around Galway. One of my favorite sites is Inchagoill island on Lough Corrib, just a few miles north of us. Legend tells us that Patrick was banished here for a time by local Druids. The name of the place means "island of the stranger." The island is now uninhabited, but there is a stone church at the site where Patrick's fifth-century wooden church would have been, as well as a marker stone where his nephew and navigator is buried; it is one of the oldest Christian markers we have. There is a later twelfth-century church nearby as well.

Seeking out this strangeness and exile was at the heart of the monastic call. In going to the places that make us feel uncomfortable and staying with our experience rather than running away, they cracked themselves open to receive the Spirit in new ways.

But in this seeking out of strangeness and risk, one does long for a sense of protection or safety within the arms of the divine. As we explored at the start of this chapter, St. Patrick's lorica prayer was one type of prayer to invoke this protection and a reminder of the sacred presence always with us already.

Call upon St. Patrick to support you in finding protection from harmful energies and elements. Ask him to encircle you with God's loving presence.

Scripture Reflection by John Valters Paintner

Lectio Divina

> You who live in the shelter of the Most High,
>> who abide in the shadow of the Almighty,
> will say to the LORD, "My refuge and my fortress;
>> my God, in whom I trust."
> For he will deliver you from the snare of the fowler
>> and from the deadly pestilence;
> he will cover you with his pinions,
>> and under his wings you will find refuge;
>> his faithfulness is a shield and buckler.
> You will not fear the terror of the night,
>> or the arrow that flies by day,
> or the pestilence that stalks in darkness,
>> or the destruction that wastes at noonday.
>> —Psalm 91:1–6

Biblical Context

Tradition teaches that King David is the sole author of the book of Psalms. Modern scholarship puts considerable doubt on this notion due to language, historical context, and other reasons. I prefer to think of the psalms as inspired by David and not get into who wrote which specific psalm. It's a debate better left to those with more experience in this particular area of biblical studies than I have.

Regardless of the actual author of Psalm 91, it is written by one who has sought shelter in the Temple under God's protection. The Chosen People believed the Ark of the Covenant to be God's throne and the Temple to be God's dwelling place on earth. Where else would one seek sanctuary, other than within the protective walls of God's house?

Despite the cold, hard stone of the actual structure itself, the feeling is one of the loving embrace of a parent. This overconfidence in the protective walls of the Temple and the walls of Jerusalem, rather than adherence to the covenant within, is ultimately disastrous during the Babylonian invasion, but the psalmist has faith that no harm will befall him or her.

Personal Reflection

There is something very comforting about being surrounded. Infants love to be wrapped up. Special coats or tight-fitting shirts soothe dogs with anxiety. And I don't know about you, but even when it is very hot at night, I find it difficult to get comfortable and sleep if I don't at least have a bedsheet in which to curl up.

Sometimes we need the reassurance of walls or blankets or the presence of others to feel safe.

I know Christine and I feel very safe in our new home. We're on the top floor of an apartment building with a front door that is not right on the street. Delivery people with our actual address and detailed instructions have difficulty finding us. I think it unlikely a burglar could be bothered to find us. However, this means friends and invited guests have difficulty locating us as well.

That's one of the great conundrums of life: the only way to completely protect ourselves from life is to block it out completely, which is no life at all. And so despite the inconvenience and our reluctance, we venture out to help bring people into our comfy nests. In fact, the only reason they are comfy nests is because they include our circle of friends.

And so while Christine and I feel very fortunate to have a lovely new home, what makes it a true blessing are the friends who grace it with their presence. We are encircled by a wall of love that does not block out the world, because it is of the world. It is made up of family and friends who support us and challenge us. It is the Communion of Saints embodied. Each and every one of them is a gift from God who, together, encircle and protect us.

The Practice of Encircling or Encompassing

The word *caim* comes from the Irish Gaelic meaning "protection" or "encompassing," and is a prayer similar in function to the lorica, used to invoke divine protection or the care of a saint. It is an invisible circle drawn around oneself and one's body to serve as a reminder of God's protection and the presence of love and safety even in difficult times. It is a way to pray physically and integrate this with the heart's longings. Philip Sheldrake writes that "such protective prayers of blessing for boundaries, whether of places or around individuals, were quite common in the Celtic tradition. They are almost certainly adaptations of pre-Christian rites. Although the forms differed, such prayers often involved blessings and signs of protection being made to all four quarters of the world, then to the earth and finally to the skies above."[4]

In praying a caim, extend the right index finger toward the ground, and then turn slowly clockwise (or sunwise), facing all four directions and drawing an imaginary circle, which creates the protective enclosure. Turning sunwise is essential, as it shows you are moving in harmony with cosmic forces rather than against them. You acknowledge that you are encircled already by creation not of your own making, moving in its own rhythms and seasons.

You can pause at each of the four directions and ask the spirit or energy of that direction to help support you in this protection. Once you complete the circle, the circle travels with you. (This prayer was often said before embarking on pilgrimage.)

You can extend this circle beyond yourself and include your family, your community, your country, the earth. It is an intentional act of calling forth protection for the whole community you are a part of. This is one of the earliest known caim prayers, attributed to St. Columcille: "Bless to me the sky that is above me. Bless to me the ground that is beneath me. Bless to me the friends who are around me. Bless to me the love of the Three, deep within me and encircling me. Amen."[5]

These prayers are not an attempt to manipulate God to provide protection. The purpose is more to remember the continual presence of the divine in every direction—north, east, south, and west—as well as within, between, beneath, and above. We receive that protection when we bring it consciously into our lives, when we step with intention into this encircling presence of God. We draw on the sacred energy to help us face the fears within and around us.

We know the directions were sacred and vital to the Celtic monks because all of their churches in Ireland were built with an east-west orientation. The altar always faces the east window because this is the direction of the dawn and the Resurrection. Often there would be high crosses outside the church in each of the four directions to mark out the sanctuary space and draw a circle of protection around the building and those praying in it.

Photography Exploration: Images of God in Every Direction

You are invited to go on a contemplative walk with camera in hand again. Begin by centering yourself. Bring your awareness into your heart center and go out with an openness to receive what comes. I invite you to pause regularly on your walk when something shimmers or you feel moved to linger for a moment. You can receive that moment with your camera, but then turn a quarter-turn to the right, receive a photo there; then make another quarter-turn, and receive a photo; one final quarter turn, and one more photo there.

What do you discover when you look for the divine presence in every direction? We are sometimes so captivated by what is in front of us that we miss what is to the side of or behind us. Spend some time with these images and see what you notice and discover.

Writing Exploration: Lorica Prayer

Read over St. Patrick's lorica prayer again, and write your own prayer of encircling and shielding that reminds you of the divine presence without and around you at all moments. Write about how you discover the divine in each direction—east, south, west, north, skywards, earthwards, within. From what do you need protection in your life right now? Include this in your prayer.

Closing Blessing

I offer you a poem I wrote inspired by the story of St. Patrick climbing the holy mountain and spending forty days there in prayer, a time I imagine there must have been much discomfort as well as revelation. He sought God up high and knew God down low as well.

What have you been discovering about your own need for boundaries and a sacred no?

Holy Mountain

I want to climb the holy mountain
ascend over weight of stone
and force of gravity, follow the
rise of a wide and cracked earth
toward eternal sky,
take measured steps across the sharp path,
rest often to catch my heavy breath.

I want to hear the silence of stone and stars,
lie back on granite's steep rise
face to silver sky's glittering points
where I can taste the galaxies
on my tongue, communion of fire,
then stand on the summit and
look out at the laboring world.

I want to witness Earth's slow turning
with early light brushing over me,
a hundred hues
of grey, pink, gold,
speckles of Jackson Pollock light,

then ribbons of mist floating
like white streamers of surrender.

I want to look back down the trail
as if over my past, forgive a thousand tiny
and tremendous transgressions
because now all that matters
is how small I feel under the sky;
even the sparrow hawk takes no notice of me,
how enlarged I feel by knowing this smallness.

I want to be like St. Patrick,
climb the holy mountain full of
promise and direction and knowing,
forty days of fasting aloft among clouds

until my body no longer hungers
and something inside is satisfied
and my restless heart says here,
no longer dreaming of other peaks.[6]

chapter 7

The practice of walking the Rounds

One of the first Irish practices we were introduced to when we moved here and began visiting sacred sites was the practice of walking the rounds in a sunwise direction. To walk sunwise means clockwise to our more modern minds, but of course the sun was first. To walk the rounds sunwise means to walk in harmony with cosmic forces. The number of rounds varies, but generally you would walk either a single round, the sacred number of three rounds, or a full seven or twelve rounds, also holy numbers.

You walk the rounds around various sacred monuments, such as a holy well, a church ruin, a grave, certain trees, a cross, or sometimes a pile of stones or a cairn. Many sacred sites have a series of these monuments, and the idea is to walk the rounds around each of them in a certain order. This is a kind of prescribed pilgrimage experience, and there are many places in Ireland that still host these walks in community on various feast days. At each of these stations, the tradition is to walk *deiseal*, which means in a sunwise direction around each one. Certain prayers are said, often traditional prayers such as the Our Father and the Hail Mary, but many people visit now and offer their own prayers as they walk or let it be a silent meditation.

There are still many of these pilgrimage stations throughout Ireland, and when we bring out pilgrimage groups out to the holy sites, we often invite pilgrims to walk in this intentional way. This isn't a mindless exercise of superstition but instead a sacred invitation to bring ourselves fully present to this moment and to walk with full mindfulness and affectionate awareness.

The Celtic peoples loved spiral designs, as obvious from their artwork. I think these rounds serve a similar purpose to walking a labyrinth. There is a deep understanding that walking embodies our prayer, and walking in a circle has a way of moving our brains out of their desired linear course.

Rounds and Discernment

When we are discerning steps in life, we often want the next best step to appear, if not the entire path clearly ahead. But discernment in this tradition is more like a spiraling inward and a deep attentiveness to what is happening in the moment rather than a clear-cut path. We have to let go of the map and directions and move slowly inward, circling and waiting. Walking the rounds invites us to live more intuitively and organically.

Joseph Campbell offers these wise words: "We must be willing to get rid of the life we've planned, so as to have the life that is waiting for us."[1] When I went to graduate school to earn a PhD, I fully expected to leave the program and apply to work at a university. I had certain clear ideas about what I "should" do now that I had spent so many years studying for the important piece of paper that gave me a certain authority and many thousands of dollars in student loans. The *shoulds* included a full-time position at a university with benefits and a retirement plan. So I found myself in the unfamiliar place of trying to release my planning tendencies and recognize how plans give me a feeling of control and certainty. The invitation was to step into the unknown, into the discomfort we have been exploring together.

Then several things happened in my life. My husband and I visited friends in Seattle on vacation and absolutely fell in love with the city right on the spot. I remember the moment we looked at each other to see if the other was smitten as well.

Choosing the place first and job second definitely limits your options, but we had fallen in love with a landscape and were willing to give it a try. I started working at Seattle University part-time as an adjunct, and they were very generous with giving me classes to teach. I kept thinking if I had a secure and steady source of income I would be free of the financial fears that had haunted me all those years living month-to-month in graduate school. I would be able to devote the rest of my time to writing and art, my first passions.

Then my mother died two months after we moved. That time of deep grief began a midlife journey that moved me toward stunning clarity in my life around what was most life-giving. I started paying even more attention to my dreams. I began trusting my hunger to write and to make art in a more sustained way. I fell into my longing for spaciousness and silence.

I initiated conversations with John about what our life would look like if I weren't earning a full- or even part-time income, and we made efforts to live more simply so I could spend more time doing what I love and less time beholden to institutions. I love teaching, but I find that as a strong introvert, a little bit is enough to energize me. Too much and I have little energy left for anything else.

This began a long journey where my own prayer and spiritual life became a movement toward less planning how I want my life to look and more listening for the shape my life wants to take organically. John O'Donohue writes about this in his book *Anam Cara*:

> Spirituality is the art of transfiguration. We should not force ourselves to change by hammering our lives into any predetermined shape. We do not need to operate according to the idea of a predetermined program or plan for our lives. Rather, we need to practice a new art of attention to the inner rhythm of our days and lives. . . . If you work with a different rhythm, you will come easily and naturally home to yourself. Your soul knows the geography of your own destiny. Your soul alone has the map of your future, therefore you can trust this indirect, oblique side of yourself. . . . If you attend to yourself and seek to come into your presence, you will find exactly the right rhythm for your life.[2]

He is talking about honoring the voice and rhythms of the Deep Self, that place where the mystics tell us God dwells. I began having dreams that encouraged me to have an even more playful and spacious understanding of discernment. I joined a dream group and mined the rich veins of gold rising in my sleep. I started trusting my intuition more, my sense of the rightness of something even if it didn't seem like the logical thing to do. I listened for the ways my body wanted to pray and allowed myself to enter in the changing landscape of my emotional life. When I started to feel stuck, I embraced my stuckness and allowed for fallow moments. My images of God began to explode much wider than they ever had before.

My prayers were to listen to the shape and rhythm my life wanted to move into and to trust that this would be enough, with "enough" countering a whole host of fears around money and accomplishments needed for ego-boosting, to assure myself all those years of studying meant something. I began to realize, too, that the first half of my life journey had been primarily focused on book learning and this second half would be a journey of fully embracing my own wisdom and experience.

Of course this experience and transformation also sowed the seeds for our move to Europe nine years following. By then I was much more willing and even eager to release my own plans and step into the adventure my heart desired. When we allow the ripening to happen in its own time, we discover that what emerges is much truer to our own hearts than anything our minds can concoct.

St. Sourney of Drumacoo

Sourney is one of the female Irish saints from the sixth century, and while there is little written about her, two of my favorite sacred sites are dedicated to her memory. The first is on the island of Inishmore and is said to be her hermitage. There is a signpost off the main road, but the path is quite overgrown with brambles. The chapel itself is in disrepair—only part of it remains—but standing inside you can imagine the saint there, seeking the grace of silence and solitude on the holy island. When you step out the front door, you see the wide sea beyond.

Later in her life, she was called to Drumacoo, near the village of Kilcolgan, about a half hour from Galway City. A large church ruin appears behind the cemetery with a more modern mausoleum attached to the side. Further back is the holy well of St. Sourney. When we first visited it, the well was quiet overgrown and a bit hard to access without tripping over stones and tree roots. But people from the community and the Office of Public Works have since cleared it up beautifully. There is a now a set of stones in a circle to mark off the opening of the holy well and a clear path around it for walking the rounds, which we do on our own visits and when we bring pilgrims there. In the Celtic imagination, the holy well is the source of all life bubbling up from within the earth. To reach into those waters is to reach into the source of life itself. It is considered one of the portals between worlds as well, between what is seen and unseen.

We don't know the details of St. Sourney's life and service, but I love that despite this, two beautiful sites have persisted for more than fifteen hundred years to carry her spirit forward. I imagine her walking the rounds in these places, mulling over her own discernment questions and life trajectory. While her written story did not persist, the land holds her memory in stone and water.

Call upon St. Sourney to be with you as you travel life's path. Ask her to show you the spiral way inward and to help release you of your desire for a direct route to answers.

Scripture Reflection by John Valters Paintner

Lectio Divina

> Moses was keeping the flock of his father-in-law Jethro, the priest of Midian; he led his flock beyond the wilderness, and came to Horeb, the mountain of God. There the angel of the Lord appeared to him in a flame of fire out of a bush; he looked, and the bush was blazing, yet it was not consumed. Then Moses

said, "I must turn aside and look at this great sight, and see why the bush is not burned up." When the LORD saw that he had turned aside to see, God called to him out of the bush, "Moses, Moses!" And he said, "Here I am." Then he said, "Come no closer! Remove the sandals from your feet, for the place on which you are standing is holy ground." He said further, "I am the God of your father, the God of Abraham, the God of Isaac, and the God of Jacob." And Moses hid his face, for he was afraid to look at God.

—Exodus 3:1–6

Biblical Context

In the opening verses of the book of Exodus, we learn that the twelve sons of Jacob have moved to Egypt and, over the generations, multiplied into the twelve tribes of Israel. Fearing their growing numbers, a new pharaoh—who did not remember how Joseph had saved Egypt from a severe famine and made the country a great power in the region—enslaved the "foreigners" in his midst. The pharaoh even went so far as to order the midwives Shiphrah and Puah to secretly kill all the male Israelite babies. But they refused to become the pharaoh's assassins and found a way to disobey. Not to be deterred, the pharaoh then abandoned any attempt at subtlety and ordered the slaughter of all male Israelite babies.

Enter the infant Moses, whose mother was apparently so desperate to save her young son's life that she placed him in a basket and floated him down the Nile River. But appearances can be deceiving. It was not just blind luck that floated Moses past the pharaoh's daughter as she just happened to be bathing with a large entourage in her usual spot. It was not just happenstance that Moses's sister, Miriam, was there just as the princess wondered aloud where she might fight a wet nurse to feed this child she had found. And it was more than just a coincidence that the woman Miriam suggested was Moses's own mother. This small scene from scripture is often read as a lucky accident, but to me it reads as a well-organized con game.

Moses's life was spared by two clever midwives who refused to become the pharaoh's executioners and by Moses's clever family, who tricked the pharaoh into bring up Moses in the safety of the palace.

One night while visiting his kin, Moses came to the rescue of one of his fellow Israelites, who was being beaten by an Egyptian overseer. Moses killed the abuser and buried the body in the sand. But word quickly spread of Moses's deed, and he fled rather than face prosecution.

When he came across a desert oasis, Moses witnessed a woman being denied access to the well. Once again Moses's sense of justice led him to action, and he helped the woman, whom he soon married. In seemingly no time, Moses had started a family and begun a whole new life as a nomadic shepherd.

Moses was minding his own business, or more accurately, minding the herd of his father-in-law, when God called to him in the form of a shrub that burned but was not consumed. At first, Moses hid his face in fear. But God would not be ignored and called out again to Moses.

God told Moses that the cries of the Israelites for justice had been heard. God then instructed Moses to return to the land of his birth, where he would be God's spokesperson for the rescue of the Chosen People and return them to the Promised Land.

Moses was reluctant, but God is persistent.

Personal Reflection

Despite being the great, primordial prophet of the Hebrew Scriptures, Moses acted like a whiny little child in this passage. He clearly did not want to return to Egypt. He did not want to leave the comfort of his new life to return to the place where he was wanted for murder. And this first interaction between Moses and God consisted of a series of lame excuses from the future leader of the Israelite people.

At first, Moses tried to play the humble card. He claimed that he was a nobody, as if he wasn't uniquely qualified to be the spokesman for his kin. Moses was born an Israelite but raised in the pharaoh's palace. He knew all the political players and how the game worked.

He was the perfect bridge between these two interwoven cultures, and Moses was assured that God would be at his side the whole way.

But the whining didn't stop there. Because next, Moses tried to be clever and said that the Israelites wouldn't believe him because he didn't know God's name, knowing full well that God had not yet revealed this information to anyone. But Moses was put in his place when he became the first person to learn the name of God: Yahweh.

Moses then suggested that the Israelites still might not believe him, so God gave him three different signs and wonders to convince the people. And while one might think that would have shut Moses up, the excuses continued.

Finally, Moses resorted to bad mouthing God's choice by stating that he was not eloquent and wouldn't know what to say. God reminded Moses that all he had to do was repeat God's words. When even that didn't seem to be enough for him, God told Moses that his brother Aaron would accompany him and abruptly ended the conversation, sending Moses on his way back to Egypt.

The religious practice is not called "walking the round." "Rounds" is plural for a reason. Some of us, occasionally, are blessed with instant retention of information. Most of us need time and repetition before things sink in to our consciousness.

It took Moses longer than it should have to accept his role in the Exodus story. We shouldn't be too hard on ourselves when we follow in his footsteps. Just as Moses went around and around with God at the burning bush, we often need several rounds before we are ready to proceed.

Even after the Israelites were free, it took Moses and the Israelites forty years of wandering to get back to their ancestral Promised Land. Geographically, they knew exactly where they were and where they were headed. Still, they went in circles for a long time because they needed that time to prepare. They would not have been successful if they had attempted to jump straight to the end.

We cannot be so impatient for the destination that we arrive before we are ready.

Leading thousands from Egypt to the Promised Land over the course of forty years may seem a bit overwhelming. But the Israelites' long journey through the wilderness began with a few simple steps by Moses. Rather than being overwhelmed by the magnitude of the journey ahead, like Moses, we need to be reminded that we are already on sacred ground. All we need do to begin the journey is to remove our sandals in recognition that where we stand is already holy.

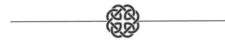

The Practice of Walking the Rounds

The tradition of pilgrimage in Ireland is an ancient one. There are many trails and paths that have been considered sacred for hundreds, if not thousands, of years.

One of the more ancient Irish practices of pilgrimage is *deiseal*, which, as mentioned at the start of this chapter, means to walk in a sunwise direction. This is done in holy places, and often there is a series of pilgrim stations—a series of cairns, a holy well, a cross, a chapel or sanctuary space—and each of these invites a circumambulation of generally one, three, five, seven, or twelve rounds, always in harmony with creation and the rhythms of the universe.

The purpose of walking the rounds is multifaceted. The first is that walking helps to slow us down. The poet Wallace Stevens once said "Perhaps the truth depends upon a walk around the lake."[3] We allow ourselves to arrive fully in a sacred place, both body and soul, and ask permission to be there and receive the gifts offered.

The second purpose is that walking in a circular manner helps to move us out of linear ways of thinking. It allows us to rest into the spiral nature of time and see things from a new perspective. Pilgrimage is never a straight, step-by-step journey but one of continual unfolding and listening to wisdom arising from dreams and nature.

Another purpose is that walking helps us to bless the earth with our feet so that our whole being becomes a prayer. Instead of walking to get somewhere, as we might when journeying to a particular place, walking the rounds invites us to continue journeying in place.

While walking the rounds, traditional prayers such as the Hail Mary and Our Father might be said, but any prayers of the heart are welcome. You might repeat a mantra or sing a meditative song.

Consider finding a holy place to walk around. It might be a sunwise journey around a favorite tree, or inside your church, or even around the edges of a labyrinth nearby. If you are stuck indoors because of severe weather, simply allow a few breaths to center yourself and then walk the room in gentle, sunwise circles, not trying to figure anything out but simply allowing yourself to be fully present and attentive. If a recited prayer helps, let that be your mind's focus and anchor. The breath can also be a beautiful way to return your attention again and again.

Try practicing this ancient tradition of walking the rounds while bringing yourself here and now and see what you notice or discover.

Photography Exploration: Walking the Rounds

You are invited to go on another contemplative walk. Each time something shimmers for you, I invite you to pause before you receive the photo. If possible, walk the rounds three times around whatever has captivated your attention. Let yourself arrive, ask permission to receive a photo, and then see if walking the rounds changes your relationship to whatever this is. Let this process slow you down first and arrive rather than reaching for the camera immediately to capture the moment. Receive images only once you feel you have arrived and been welcomed by the place.

What do you notice or discover when you slow yourself down like this?

Writing Exploration: Haiku

When we lead our writing retreats on the island of Inishmore, we go out one morning to the sacred site right behind our bed and breakfast; it is dedicated to St. Colman. We walk the rounds together three times around the ancient ruins, and then we spend time in silence writing haiku.

I invite you to begin this writing exploration by going somewhere out in nature; it could be a city park or somewhere wilder. Walk rounds yourself around a tree or boulder or other place in the landscape. Then notice where your attention is drawn and write a series of poems in the form of haiku. Haiku are traditionally seventeen syllables: five syllables on the first line, seven on the second, and five on the third. Keep in mind that while poetry has many rules, the first one is to feel free to break the rules. Don't stay too rigidly attached to the seventeen syllables if fifteen or twenty express the moment better.

The purpose of the haiku is really to pay attention to a moment in time, capturing a fleeting instant, usually in nature. This is a beautiful way to sit in creation and notice small happenings around you. You can also carry pen and paper with you in your day and pause regularly. Allow some deep breaths and just pay attention to what is happening right then before you. You might even set your phone alarm to go off at regular intervals as a way of calling your attention back to this moment now. Then write a haiku inspired by what you notice.

This can also be a way to reflect on your contemplative walk experience. Consider writing some haiku from the photos that called out to you for more attention.

Closing Blessing

We all have times in our lives when our own inner holy well needs tending and replenishment. When the waters don't flow as abundantly anymore because we have become depleted. Too often we look to the outside world as the source of our renewal, awaiting its permission and encouragement, which never comes. When we recognize ourselves as branches of a much deeper source, we can return to the place where our nourishment comes.

How are you being invited to let go of a linear path forward and allow a more organic approach to life?

st. sourney's well

Gentian blue sky,
dandelion seed clouds play
hide and seek with the sun.

Brightly colored ribbons hang
from hawthorn, old party
streamers from branches, banners

of longing: a prayer for healing
the great divide of the heart,
or a beloved consumed by cancer.

Or simply an echo of the psalmist's
ancient cry, "How long, O God?"
into the vast and thunderous silence.

Walking the rounds, always sunwise,
slowly arriving, footsteps bless
the ground, saying I am here.

No pronouncements in reply,
no choruses of Alleluia.
Only moss and streams and birdsong,

only knowing that life still
burgeons here on the edges of
our own landscapes of loss.

I plunge in my hands.

chapter 8

The practice of Learning by Heart

When John and I bring groups on our pilgrimage outings, they are often entranced by two of our guides in particular—Tony Kirby at the Burren and Pius Murray on the island of Inisheer, who each recite memorized poems several times during our walk together. Indeed, it seems to be very much part of the ongoing Irish tradition to commit poems to heart, to bring them intimately into oneself for remembering. The words seem knit into our guides' consciousness in ways that makes the speaking of the words feel transcendent.

In the Hebrew Scriptures, there are many passages that describe the new covenant as written not on stone but in the hearts of the people. There is a shift from a list of rules to follow to a true experience of conversion. The motivation to do good things in the world comes from an internal motivation rather than an external one. This speaks to me of the ripening wisdom of a people and how God speaks to us in different ways at different times. The beauty is that it says God is willing to try different approaches with us. We may need to hear the message in one form at a certain moment of our lives, but over time, it will come again to us in different ways.

While the Irish monks are known for their gifts of illuminating sacred texts, books were rare and valuable, so they would have had to learn many scripture passages by heart to be able to pray with them. This was a continuation of the older Druidic tradition, a primarily oral culture where memorization rather than writing was prized. Oliver Davies says that a key characteristic "of original Celtic religion was its orality. It is probably inevitable that a primal religion, rooted in a particular people and locality, will shun the written word since this may seem to compromise the privileged position of the priestly caste who are charged with maintaining the native lore through an oral medium."[1]

The Irish monks would have sung the psalms throughout each day as a central part of their prayer. They were immersed in this poetry and ancient call to see God active in the whole world. When you speak and sing these words, you join in with these ancient prayers as well. They likely would have memorized all 150 of them as their days were so intertwined with their imagery. We know how important the psalms were even to the hermits from the story of St. Kevin, whose psalter fell in the lake and his friend the otter went to rescue it for him.

Theologian of Irish spirituality Peter O'Dwyer describes the reciting of the psalms as an essential aspect of the Irish monk's life. These were said "along with postures of standing or sitting or reading or praying them by heart."[2] In addition, in communities, two monks would recite the psalms throughout each night. This rhythm of the liturgy was intimately connected to the rhythms of the earth, and so the monk was encircled and embraced by the rise and fall of each day and each year.

Many of us might have experienced at school the assignment to memorize certain things, ranging from the periodic table of elements to lines for a play. Sadly, it wasn't often done as a way to cultivate a love for something but instead as a practical endeavor. Unless we have a true heart connection, we aren't likely to see the value in what we are doing. We are so accustomed to having the texts we need readily available that I often wonder what it would be like if those words didn't live on paper or digitally but were inscribed on our hearts. How might we be shaped by their invitation in new ways?

John O'Donohue describes this way of remembering as keeping things in the temple of memory: "The Celtic stories suggest that time as the rhythm of soul has an eternal dimension where everything is gathered and minded. Here nothing is lost. This is a great consolation: The happenings in your life do not disappear. Nothing is ever lost or forgotten. Everything is stored within your soul in the temple of memory."[3] I love this image of learning by heart as a storing in the inner temple.

Discernment and the Heart

I have already mentioned how certain lines of poetry have met me at a particular season of my life and served to support and inspire me or move me toward new ways of seeing. The line "What you can plan is too small for you to live" from David Whyte was definitely such a line that, as it lived in my heart, encouraged me to release my grasp from planning and wanting to control the outcome of my discernment.

In a time of grief, I was reading Jane Hirshfield's poem "Lake and Maple," and the line "In the still heart, that refuses nothing" shimmered brightly for me. The poem is about autumn and surrender. I was suddenly aware of all the ways my heart was refusing life, refusing the truth of my experience, wanting things to be different than they were. Whenever I found myself trying to block the waves of sorrow I was experiencing, I would remember this line, and it helped to create a gateway within me where I was able to welcome in the fullness of what was coming through.

In another season of my life, Mary Oliver's poem "Almost a Conversation" found its way into my heart. In the poem, she imagines the wisdom an otter might have to offer us and ends with a pondering: "He wonders, morning after morning, that the river / is so cold and fresh and alive, and still / I don't jump in." I was enchanted by the way she entered into the otter's way of being, and something about that sense of the cold and fresh flowing water of the river invited me to consider places in my own life where I was holding back. Each time I walked by the river Corrib, which runs through the heart of Galway, those words came back to me, calling me to consider where I needed to press forward in my life.

Discernment is an act of the heart, a way of listening with more than the mind—with the body and the intuition as well. When we discern, we are making space for new revelation to arrive without needing to force it. This is the soul's slow ripening. Often that wisdom or insight arrives in the form of words from others. Perhaps you are sitting in church on a Sunday and suddenly the scripture verse comes alive in a new way because of how it is being read or because you are new in that moment, receiving it from a different vantage point.

Poetry has a way of expressing things of the heart so beautifully, of holding the paradox of life and inviting us into a contemplation of the mysteries. When discerning how your own soul is unfolding, keep an ear attuned to poetry or other words that seem to call you to a deepened sense of yourself and of the divine presence in the midst of your listening.

St. Brendan the Navigator

Brendan is probably one of the best-known Irish saints after Brigid and Patrick. He lived from 486 to 578 and spent several early years with St. Ita, whom we will explore in the last chapter of this book. There are several sites in the west of Ireland connected to Brendan, including the Cathedral at Clonfert, Mount Brandon in Dingle, and the monastery he founded at Annaghdown near Galway, where he spent the last few days of his life.

The "Navigator," or "Voyager," is his commonly known title because his life was defined by his seven-year-long journey across the sea to find the island promised to the saints. He would have visited the island of Inishmore off the coast of county Galway to receive a blessing from St. Enda before embarking on his journey, and I relish knowing I have walked and sailed on some of the same landscape as he did.

Brendan heard the call to search for this mythical island; it was revealed in a dream by an angel who said that he would be with him and guide him there. Brendan brought along a group of fellow monks for community and searched for seven years sailing in circles, visiting many of the islands again and again. Each year he celebrated Easter Mass on the back of a whale. And each year he visited the island of the birds, where white-feathered creatures would sing the psalms with his monks. Only when his eyes were opened did he see that the paradise he sought was right with him.

Brendan and his monks would have known many of the scriptures by heart, certainly the psalms that were at the center of their daily prayers even as they journeyed by sea for many years. They still paused regularly to chant those ancient words together, to remind themselves of whom and why they were seeking.

His journey is an allegory of spiritual transformation and the soul's seeking to live and respond to the world from an experience of inner transfiguration; it contains themes of Brendan's waiting, anticipating, striving, searching, and seeing from a deeper perspective. The heart of the voyage asks us: What needs to change for the island promised to the saints to be recognized? What is the way required through both illuminated and shadowy interior landscapes? Are we able to stay present through moments of solace, ease, and joy, as well as the anxiety, fear, and sometimes terror that comes when we let go of all that is familiar to follow our heart's calling? Can we see the difficult journey as a passage of initiation?

The longest journey seems to be the letting go of the expectations, the assumptions, the woundedness; all of the ways we seek just what we are looking for rather than what is waiting to be revealed. In many ways, this is a continuation of our practice of yielding, which we explored in the last chapter, and releasing our expectations, following the current of where life is carrying us.

Call upon St. Brendan in the coming days to help you remember things of the heart.

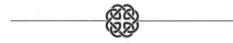

Scripture Reflection by John Valters Paintner

Lectio Divina

> The days are surely coming, says the LORD, when I will make a new covenant with the house of Israel and the house of Judah. It will not be like the covenant that

I made with their ancestors when I took them by the hand to bring them out of the land of Egypt—a covenant that they broke, though I was their husband, says the LORD. But this is the covenant that I will make with the house of Israel after those days, says the LORD: I will put my law within them, and I will write it on their hearts; and I will be their God, and they shall be my people. No longer shall they teach one another, or say to each other, "Know the LORD," for they shall all know me, from the least of them to the greatest, says the LORD; for I will forgive their iniquity, and remember their sin no more.

—Jeremiah 31:31–34

Biblical Context

To understand Jeremiah's New Covenant, one must first examine the Old Covenant.

After God rescued the Israelites from bondage in Egypt, they were led to the holy mountain where they received the Ten Commandments (the first of 613 rules in total) to follow in gratitude for their deliverance from slavery—and that "after" is of great importance. Adherence to the covenant did not get them into God's good graces. Obedient observance of the commandments did not earn them an afterlife or even blessings in the present one. It was thanksgiving for their life and liberty, which God had already freely given to them. Keeping the covenant is how the Israelites, down through the generations, showed gratitude for their many blessings.

The commandments were famously written on stone tablets that eventually were placed inside the ark of the covenant, a large crate topped with angelic statues and covered in gold. This ark itself became a sacred object, as much as its contents. The Israelites paraded it before them in ceremonies and even into battle.

The ark eventually got a special tent or tabernacle for when it was not being carried from place to place. Then, King David gave the ark and the tabernacle a permanent home on what became known as the

Temple Mount in Jerusalem. His son, King Solomon, soon built the Temple around the ark. And there it stayed for generations, a symbol of God's throne on earth, within "the holy of holies" of the one Temple in the holy City of David.

The Israelites came to believe that the mere presence of the ark of the covenant itself was what protected them from invasion and destruction. This belief was reinforced when the Assyrian invasion collapsed at the city walls.

Jeremiah and other prophets tried to warn their fellow Israelites that it was not the container but the contents that saved them. But the contents had been sealed away for safekeeping for so long—in a special box, within a special room, in a special Temple, on a holy mount, within a walled city on a hill—that most didn't know what was written inside. The tablets were kept from prying eyes. Only the chief priest was allowed to go near. And I mean *only*. On the rare occasions when the priest would enter the inner sanctum, a special cord was tied around his ankle. For if he were to collapse while inside, no one else was allowed to go in and rescue him. They'd have to drag him out using the cord.

Personal Reflection

Is it any wonder that the covenant had been forgotten? Was there not a need for a New Covenant, even before the Ark of the Covenant was taken and/or destroyed by the conquering Babylonians?

What Jeremiah is talking about is actually a renewal of the old covenant: "I will be your God and you shall be my people." The only thing that would change was the accessibility of the covenant. It would no longer be the exclusive domain of the high priest. There would be no more redundant barriers between it and the people. Everyone would carry it within themselves. Jeremiah's New Covenant would not require a special pilgrimage or elaborate ritual to get to. People would already have it.

One might think of it as a renewal of the covenant, like the way a couple might renew their wedding vows. Christine and I recently renewed our wedding vows among friends on Inishmore. It wasn't because our marriage was in trouble. We hadn't broken the original vows, but after twenty years together, it was good to publically re-state our commitment to each other. It was a celebration of the last two decades together and a promise for the future.

Also of note is where this New Covenant is located. It's written on our hearts. But I fear our modern, scientific worldview keeps us from understanding Jeremiah's metaphor.

You see, ancient people tended to not have the same basic medi-cal and biological understanding that even the average non-scientist has today. Ironically, our ancestors did not know what the brain did. Their best collective guess was that it somehow cooled the blood. The Egyptians, who took such great care in preserving in special containers all the internal organs of the dead pharaohs, literally scooped the brains out through the nose and threw them away.

The Israelites, like most of their neighboring cultures, tended to think of memories as stored in the heart. This means that when Jere-miah speaks of the New Covenant "written on our hearts," he is not taking about "being in love with God" or "feeling spirituality"; he is talking about knowing the covenant on an intellectual level. More than just memorizing, but understanding.

And all of that requires time, repetition and time.

The Practice of Learning by Heart

Of all the practices in this book, this is the one I struggle with the most. My memory for facts and specific words is not very good. I can remember lines of poems that have touched my heart, but full poems often seem out of my grasp. I have a deep longing to be able to recite my own poems from memory, to be able to draw on my heart's remembering to speak aloud the words that have been in-spired in me.

I do think that each of us has some memory functions that are stronger than others. But wherever you stand with learning things by heart or if you have negative memories from childhood of being forced to recite dry verse, see if you might invite yourself into a new relationship with words through this practice.

Begin by finding just two lines—whether of a poem or scripture text—that are shimmering for you these days.

One line might be easy to remember, while adding the second offers some additional challenge. Spend some time each morning with these lines, repeating them gently to yourself then and throughout the day.

Each day add one more line to remember, so that slowly, over the span of a week's time, you have built yourself up to seven lines.

You might also bring the written text of the poem or scripture on a walk with you and recite the words as you walk, letting them fall into the rhythm of your step and become embodied. If you stumble on a line, simply look at the paper and find your way again. When we learn by heart while walking, we are embodying the rhythm of the words into our muscles and bones.

Photography Exploration: Framing

For your contemplative walk, prepare yourself by centering and allowing yourself to arrive fully here in this moment of time. Pay special attention to your breath and with each exhale, see if you can physically release and yield your body. Become aware of places of tightness and holding; bring your breath to these places, and in your imagination create a sense of spaciousness. Then let your exhale be exaggerated into a sigh of release.

As you journey with camera in hand, I invite you to become aware of open spaces. These could be sky or field, open road, or seascape. Play with the element of framing; try placing whatever object is calling to you on the edge of the frame with as much open space held in the rest of the frame as possible to create some interesting tension. Framing is where we direct our attention. When we learn something by heart, we put a frame around it in our consciousness in a very particular way.

When you return home, spend time again with your images and allow each to speak in its own voice from its perspective. What wisdom do the images have to offer to you about yielding? Can they show you any places in your life where you still hold on tightly?

Writing Exploration: Finding Poems in Memory
Begin with some free writing—write down any words or phrases that you can remember from poems or scripture texts, anything that you already know by heart. See how many you can write on the page from the storehouse of memory. Each might just be a line or two; it doesn't need to be the entire text.

Once you have spent ten minutes or so with this exercise in re-membering, try rearranging the phrases on the page before you into a poem of its own. This is an adaptation of "found poetry," where you would look for words or phrases in the world and put them together into a poem. But in this exercise, the poem is found within, from the texts you already know yourself.

Closing Blessing
As we reach the end of this chapter, it seems appropriate to leave you with St. Brendan's journey once more, which inspired this poem I wrote. One of my favorite moments in his story is when they come to the island with the white birds that drape the tree so fully one can no longer see the branches. When Brendan and his monks land and begin their prayers, the birds join in with their chanting of praise. The birds also know these words by heart, and it is a beautiful image to see human and bird together, offering prayers from deep within.

What are the things you know by heart?

st. brendan and the songbirds

Imagine the hubris, searching for the saint-promised
island,
the stubbornness to continue for seven journeys around
the sun.
Each day on the rolling sea, his fellow monks
jostled and tossed by waves.

Brendan asks late one evening:
How will I know when I find what I seek?
Easter Sunday brings liturgy on the back of a whale,
but as if that weren't miracle enough, they travel
    onward.

The ship is tossed onto sand and stone.
They look up to behold a broad and magnificent
oak frosted with white birds hiding the branches
    entirely,
downy tree limbs reaching upward.

The monks stand huddled under a blue stone sky,
relieved to be on stable earth for now.
The sun descends, Vespers, rose to lavender to violet,
heralding the great night's arrival.

They release a collective sigh of contentment, the air
    expands
around them as a thousand snowy birds ascend into
    that
newly hollowed space, and throats open together,
a human-avian chorus of shared devotion to the
    ancient songs and ways.

Ever eager to journey forward, Brendan still lingers for
    fifty days
sitting in that oak cathedral, feathers scribing their own
    sacred texts.
In those moments, did the relentless seeking fall away,
sliding off like the veil hiding a bride's expectant face?[4]

chapter 9

The practice of solitude and silence

The Celtic monks were profoundly influenced by the desert tradition, and while they were not able to go to the literal desert, they sought out the wild edges and lush places of wilderness. There are many sacred places in Ireland with the word *dysert* or *disert* in the name. This is the Irish word for "desert," and it refers to a place of solitude and silence, a retreat for those who longed for a more intimate encounter with God and where attention could be cultivated with fewer distractions.

Across the landscapes of Wales and Ireland we can find more than five hundred places[1] named *dysert*, places to reclaim the desert of the heart. The Irish knew that the physical desert landscape could be found in not the lush terrain of their island but the spirit of the inner desert, the cave of the heart; the cell was found within. They felt deeply called to cultivate this interior threshold space.

David Adam in his book *Border Lands* describes them this way: "The *disert* place of retreat was set up to discover the edge of glory, to experience the beyond that is in our midst. 'Diserts' are set up not to run away from what is going on, but to experience in greater depth the reality that is about them."[2]

Carved into one of the panels on many of the Irish high crosses at the great monastic sites, you see the two old hermits, St. Antony of Egypt and St. Paul of Thebes, in the Egyptian desert. They are depicted with a raven overhead because the story about them says that a raven brought half a loaf of bread every day for St. Paul to eat, but when St. Anthony was to visit him, the bird brought a whole loaf. The bread is often depicted in a circular shape, making connections to Eucharist.

The desert tradition was shaped by those who wanted to escape the Church as it was developing after Constantine. They saw its focus on wealth and prestige and fled the cities for the desert where they believed the heart of Christian life could be cultivated through silence and solitude.

Seamus Heaney, the great Irish poet, went to visit one of the small hermit dwellings on the west coast of Ireland, and he found in the building itself a reflection of the hermit life: "Inside, in the dark of the stone, it feels as if you are sustaining a great pressure, bowing down like generations of monks who must have bowed down in meditation and reparation on that stone cold floor. . . . Coming out of the cold heart of the stone into the sunlight and dazzle of grass and sea, I felt a lift in my heart, a surge toward happiness that must have been experienced over and over again by those monks as they crossed that same threshold centuries ago."[3]

Many stories of both the desert and Celtic monks focus on their kinship with creatures, as revealed in Helen Waddell's wonderful book *Beasts and Saints*. St. Kevin is said to have had an otter that would deliver him fresh salmon from the lake below his hermit cell. St. Brigid was said to have a white cow that would produce endless milk for all her guests and visitors. These stories reveal an important dimension of living the monastic life as a living out of a new creation. Monk and animal are joined together in prayer and worship.

In his book *Christ of the Celts*, John Philip Newell writes that "in the Celtic tradition, the Garden of Eden is not a place in space and time from which we are separated. It is the deepest dimension of our being from which we live in a type of exile. It is our place of origin or genesis in God. Eden is home, but we live far removed from it."[4] The monastic life offered a way to live in awareness of this paradise, cultivated moment by moment. This reverence for the graces that solitude and silence offer is also a seeking of communion with creation and intimacy with creatures. It is a living out of a homecoming that we all seek deep within ourselves. Thomas Merton described it as the monk "living the life of the new creation in which the right relation to all the rest of God's creatures is fully restored."[5]

Solitude is not a practice just for ourselves but a practice to cultivate within each of us a greater capacity for living in communion with the world. In solitude we are able to listen more intimately for the whispers of the divine alive in each moment. We also have the space needed to wrestle with our own internal voices and become clearer about which ones we want to respond to.

Solitude and Discernment

Philip Sheldrake writes that this seeking out of a desert place is to find both "a paradise, where people may live in harmony with wild animals, and at the same time a place of trial where ascetics encounter the inner and outer demons."[6] Giving oneself over to inner work in a place free of distractions demands a great commitment to wrestling with one's inner shadows.

In the desert and wilderness we discover that God dwells within us, and we also encounter light and shadow inside. The desert and Celtic monks knew a great deal about working with the thoughts that arise when we descend toward the silence that reveals our own shadowed places. St. Kevin chose a cell on a lake near the monastery at Glendalough, where for six months the sun did not shine, and he actually put himself in the shadow as a way of staying present to this inner wrestling.

In the story of the Exodus, that great legend of liberation, the Israelites come out of Egypt and wander a very long time. They become impatient and ungrateful for what has been given to them. It is a story full of humanity in all its brokenness. This is an archetypal story of grumbling and impatience when we are called out from slavery to almost unbearable nature of freedom. To step into the wilderness is to step right out of security and comfort. Often when we are on a journey of discernment, we may begin by eagerly sitting in silence in an effort to draw near to the divine and listen for holy invitations. But over time, if we are not hearing anything, or not hearing what we want to hear, we may grow impatient and unsettled.

When John and I left Seattle for Vienna and our grand adventure, I definitely had many moments of impatience and grumbling along the way. While we were certainly not fleeing slavery, we did feel as though we were following a call toward greater interior freedom. There was much uncertainty, especially in those first few months when the immigration process in Austria for John was frustratingly slow and cumbersome. We felt blocked at every turn. Every time we received another official letter, I would hold my breath in hope this was the turning point, and then often found myself weeping as I tried to decipher what further documents we were being asked to provide.

Even after moving to Ireland and immigration going so smoothly here, I had many moments of uncertainty. It takes time to root yourself in a community and make friends. I missed my dear friends from Seattle and often felt an aching loneliness. I wanted to know for certain that this was where we were being called. I longed for intimacy and community, for people who knew my story.

I also had many moments of overflowing gratitude and a sense of the sheer rightness of things. But as is often the case in our human perspective, the times I felt the sense of exile were sharper. I did find comfort in knowing that this was the path chosen by the desert monks and, soon after, Celtic monks: the longing for immersion in wild places to crack open the securities to which we cling, to shake ourselves loose from the shackles of beholding ourselves to all that is not God, all that is not life-giving.

I knew I had come on this journey to be uncomfortable, even as I fought it often. While I harbored fantasies at times of returning to our lovely settled life in Seattle, our circle of friends, and our condo (which we had sold, so we could not return to it), I had to remind myself we were being called forth and did not know why exactly.

Now that we are settled in Ireland in a stunning landscape, new layers to our work are being revealed and I am grateful for not turning back. I was being called to stay with the silence, and the unknowing that often accompanies it, for as long as was necessary. The soul ripens slowly, not on our own desired timetable.

When we are waiting for a particular outcome, we are often filled with anxiety as we sit with the unknown. Patience calls us to remember that God's time (which is beyond our *chronos*—or clock time) is present to us in our waiting. We can experience the fullness of time in the midst of waiting for time to unfold.

St. Colman Macduagh

St. Colman lived in the sixth and seventh century in county Galway in the west of Ireland. His parents were king and queen of that region, and while his mother was pregnant, his father heard a prophecy that his newborn son would one day surpass him in fame. In a jealous rage, he had his servants throw his wife into the lake with a stone tied to her. But in a miracle, the stone floated like a cork, and so she was brought safely to shore.

Once she gave birth, two priest pilgrims wandered by, and she asked them to baptize Colman. A fountain began to gush from under an ash tree so that they would have water for the rite. Because her son was still in danger from the king, she asked the two old monks to care for him.

When he grew older, he went to spend time on the holy island of Inishmore, one of the Aran Islands, which was a center for monastic learning and spirituality. Other well-known saints who had spent time there included St. Brendan, St. Ciaran, and St. Enda.

After founding two churches there, he longed for greater solitude and silence. He went into the forest of the Burren and found a cave where he could settle. You can still visit his cave, oratory, and holy well today, and it is a very beautiful site. When we bring pilgrims there, we bless ourselves at the well and spend time sitting in silence to listen to the wisdom of wind and stone, of trees and water.

It is said that Colman also brought three creatures with him—a rooster, a mouse, and a fly. The rooster would wake him for his morning prayers. The mouse would nibble on his ear if he fell back to sleep, and the fly would help him keep his place in his book of prayers.

He lived in this dysert place for seven years in silent contemplation, allowing the wilderness to teach him. Eventually, through divine intervention, he was called back to community life where he built his monastery, Kilmacduagh (which means "church of Macduagh") near Gort. It became a large ecclesiastical site that many pilgrims sought out.

Call upon St. Colman in the coming days to help teach you the wisdom of silence and guide you into holy solitude.

Scripture Reflection by John Valters Paintner

Lectio Divina

> Then God spoke all these words: I am the LORD your God, who brought you out of the land of Egypt, out of the house of slavery; you shall have no other gods before me.
>
> —Exodus 20:1–17

Biblical Context

After all the time spent and sacrifices made by the patriarchs and matriarchs to establish themselves and their kin in the Promised Land, centuries later the Chosen People found themselves enslaved in Egypt. By the time of Moses, surely the Israelites would have had just cause to feel abandoned and forgotten.

And yet, the cry of the Israelite slaves was heard. The God of their ancestors came to rescue them. Moses was merely a spokesperson for the real hero: God. And God is quite the action hero. The story of the ten plagues reads as a divine showdown between God and the pantheon of Egyptian gods and goddesses. (At this stage of the Bible, "monotheism" was defined as the Israelites siding with their one, tribal God over all the other possible gods; belief in only one, true God developed later.) The end result of this battle of deities was that God defeated the Egyptians and led the Chosen People through the wilderness back to the Promised Land. For this, and all that God did for them, the people were extremely thankful . . . mostly.

It was not long after the last notes of Miriam's song of triumph over the Egyptians reverberated into silence that her fellow Hebrews began to complain. There seemed to be a recurring mantra throughout the forty years in the wilderness: *Thank God for our freedom, but what has God done for us lately?*

The Israelites had been slaves for so long that it was difficult for them to adjust to their freedom. They hated their enslavement, but they didn't know how to be free. There had been much to complain about in Egypt, but they had known what to expect. They hadn't liked the food the Egyptians had given them, but they had gotten it on a regular basis. They hadn't liked the way the Egyptians had treated them, but they at least had known the rules (as unjust as they were). The recently freed Israelites needed a lot of support and very clear guidelines. At their first important stop along the long route back to Canaan, Moses ascended Mount Sinai and received the *Decalogue* (meaning "ten words," referring to the Ten Commandments) from God.

After such a dramatic encounter with the God of their ancestors, who freed them and gave them the covenant, one might assume that everything after this would have been smooth sailing straight back to the Promised Land. But that's clearly not what happened. It was another forty years, a generation of wandering, of stopping and starting, of conflict, of setbacks, of retracing steps, of being lost. It wasn't that the newly freed slaves didn't know where they were or where they were headed or how best to get there. There was a major trade route between Egypt and Canaan. Even considering the fact that they probably wanted to avoid the main road, lest the Egyptians come looking for them again, there is only one reason the journey back took so long: they weren't ready.

The Israelites were spiritually lost, despite having received and accepted the covenant. After living one reality (that of slaves) for so long, they needed time to adjust to their new reality (being free

111

people). The forty years in the wilderness is often seen as a punishment for the many sins and complaints of the people, so that their children (and not they) would enter the Promised Land. But there's another way of interpreting those years: it was a necessity.

The Israelites needed to spend time away and reflect on what was unfolding before them. They needed the silence and solitude of contemplation before they could act in any positive direction.

Personal Reflection

The Decalogue begins with the justification for why the freed Hebrews and their descendants should accept not just the Ten Commandments but also the covenant itself. "If for no other reason" the expression goes "than the freedom of their ancestors," even people living centuries later should have gratefully accepted these laws.

There was no promise here of future blessing or reward. Under God's instructions, Moses did lead the people to the Holy Land, but Canaan had already been promised to the descendants of Abraham and Sarah. There certainly was no mention of an eternal afterlife. (Like the concept of monotheism, belief in an afterlife is something that evolves slowly over the many books of the Bible.) The Hebrews were not called to obey these commandments because of what God *might* do for them but because of what God *had already accomplished* for them. God brought them forth out of bondage, out of slavery, out of Egypt. That should have been enough.

But the problem the Israelites kept running into in their wilderness journey was that they were too focused on what they didn't have, without spending enough time in grateful reflection on what they already had. They kept making the same mistakes because they weren't spending any time thinking about them.

Rushing into action is not something I often do. If anything, I overthink things and then never act on them. And I know the importance of the contemplation step because when I don't stop to think is when I lose my temper and lash out at people around me.

It's what the Israelites did time and again in the wilderness. They got into a little trouble and immediately started blaming God for the predicament they were in, never pausing long enough to see how they were the cause of their woes.

When I taught the Hebrew Scriptures to teenagers, every year my students would ask me why the Israelites were so whiny and why they kept making the same mistakes.

It's a fair question. Why *didn't* the Israelites learn the lesson they just experienced?

If the book of Exodus had truly been a day-by-day diary of events, then it would have been a more legitimate question. But the whole experience was written generations later. And so the authors of Exodus are really asking this question as much to themselves during the Babylonian Exile as they did of their ancestors.

So why did it take so long for the Israelites to learn their lesson, to learn to trust in God?

The first time around, in their exodus through the wilderness, they did not stop and ponder their experience. They may have been alone for much of that time, but they were never truly quiet enough to stop and listen. They were too busy escaping or just surviving to stop and think. Their descendants, those that survived the Babylonian invasion and subsequent exile, had nothing but time. They were surrounded by their oppressors, but they used the Sabbath to carve out the silence and solitude they needed to learn their lessons, to learn them well enough to teach future generations, to teach us.

The Practice of Dysert

Is there a dysert place in your own life? Where do you go for a time of retreat? It might be a place in your own home, a retreat center nearby, a beautiful landscape where you go to restore, or a faraway place that has touched your heart with its capacity to reveal the holy.

Make a commitment to find a day sometime during the next weeks to go away for a time of silence and solitude to simply listen. You can even practice dysert at home for ten minutes each day if that is all that is available to you. Turn off any notifications from your phone or computer, tell others in your house not to disturb you, and give yourself time to sit and listen. You may not hear anything at first, or you may hear the birds outside, the whir of car engines going by, the rustle of neighbors on their way out the door. Instead of fighting these as distractions, bring the art of blessing to each of these sounds. Bless the birds, the people in their cars wherever they are headed, the neighbors whose story you may or may not know.

If you are able to take more time, I recommend starting with a retreat center where you can meet with a spiritual director. Most retreat centers have an option for a silent retreat, instead of participating in a set program. Bring your desire to grow more intimate with the divine invitation in your life.

My favorite way to go on retreat these days is to head off to a hermitage here in Ireland. There are at least three that I know of, at Glendalough in Wicklow, at Glenstal Abbey in Limerick, and at Holy Hill in Sligo. Each place is in a setting of natural beauty, and the hermitages are self-contained cottages with cooking facilities. Silence is cultivated all around. Sometimes I rent a tiny cottage somewhere out in the wilds of Connemara and create a hermitage experience for myself.

I find it helpful not to bring too many distractions. Books are wonderful, but we can use them to fill our minds with thoughts and distract from the deeper silence within. I always bring a journal and a pen and my walking boots, as long walks in the woods nourish me deeply as a part of my dysert journey.

Research the possibilities for you to create your own silent retreat experience and make a commitment in the not-too-distant future to give yourself this gift of being able to drop into a deeper place, of listening for the holy whispers, and of being present to the wrestling within.

Photography Exploration:
Finding Dysert Moments

You are invited out on another contemplative walk. As always, allow time to center yourself through breathing and bringing your awareness inward. Call to mind all that you have been pondering about going to uncomfortable places.

As you set out with camera in hand, pay special attention to those moments when you feel uncomfortable. Keep a loving and open gaze, and notice when something crosses your path that may cause a little unease. This is slightly different than our shadow work in chapter 5. You are staying close to your experience and inner responses, noticing whatever it is that creates a sense of anxiety or distance.

Unless you are being threatened in the moment, I encourage you to stay with whatever is causing this internal dissonance. Receive images with an open heart, trusting that there might be a gift here for you.

Then spend part of your walk receiving images of paradise. Pay attention to the way the world around you offers up these paradise moments to contemplate. See if you can receive images of stillness and peace.

When you return home, spend some time with your images and allow two or three to call for more attention. Write from the voices of different symbols, colors, figures, or shapes, beginning with the words "I am . . ." and see where the exploration takes you. Then allow time for dialogue between voices.

What wisdom do they have to offer you for times of waiting and uncertainty?

Writing Exploration: Acrostic Poem

I invite you to explore the acrostic form of poetry. You might begin by reviewing your writing in response to your photos and see if there is a word there that feels either surprising or unsettling. Feel free to read farther back in your journal if necessary to find a word that is shimmering to you or otherwise calling to you.

Once you have found the word, or allowed it to find you, write it vertically on a piece of paper and use each letter as the first letter of a word or line of poetry. This form is called an acrostic poem. So if your word has six letters, you will have six lines altogether, with each

line being either a single word or a phrase. Try to hold this lightly
and see where it takes you.

Closing Blessing

Solitude was an essential practice for the ancient monks, seeking out
places where they could hear more clearly. The cave where St. Colman is said to have lived as a hermit for many years is a very special
place for me. I share a poem I wrote inspired by being there.

How is silence calling to you these days?

st. colman's bed

A grief-sparked journey,
you tread porous limestone
past fields of wildflower and rock,
finally see the hawthorn tree,
guardian of the place,
who asks you to bend low

through a halo of hazel scrub
to arrive where the well comes
from a fissure in the mountain's rib
and sends forth white scarves
billowing downward past your feet
toward the sea far beyond.

Before you reach your hands into the water,
you climb a bit further to the cave
stand within, stretch your arms out, touch each side;
you think of Colman sleeping there for years
and you wonder if here he could avoid the pain
of the world or did it just echo in rock and flesh.

You imagine his companions here too,
the rooster who woke him at dawn

for prayer, the mouse nibbling his ear
when he fell back to sleep,
the fly who sat still for hours
marking his place on parchment.

Perhaps you finally scream and cry and sob,
let loose the sorrow that has burrowed its way
into sinew and tendon, release it into the open mouth
of this dark cavern, hoping Colman
or God or the spirits of this place
might hear you, until there is nothing left,

until you find yourself back at the well again trying
to drink, unable to keep up with the rush of water,
while on the branch of the rag tree overhead,
its wings damp from mist,
its apricot breast full of breath and life,
a robin sings of the beauty found in stones and thorns.

chapter 10

The practice of
seasonal cycles

The unfolding of the seasons was an overarching template for the Celtic imagination and spirit. There are significant feast days aligned with the equinoxes and solstices; there are the cross-quarter days, which are the midway points between them and were part of the harvest cycle. John O'Donohue observes that "the Celtic imagination loved the circle. It recognized how the rhythm of experience, nature, and divinity followed a circular pattern."[1]

By attuning to the rhythms of the earth, the Celtic monks allowed nature to be a wisdom guide that can teach us about life's rise and fall. Esther de Waal writes in *The Celtic Way of Prayer: The Recovery of the Religious Imagination* that

> a people who farmed and knew the pattern of the seasons, who lived close to the sea and watched the ebb and flow of tides, above all who watched the daily cycle of the sun and the changing path of the moon, brought all of this into their prayer. . . . The holding together of dark and light, cold and warmth, came naturally to a people whose whole livelihood showed death and rebirth, dying and new life, was a natural and inevitable part of their existence.[2]

The monastic way is full of respect for these sacred rhythms. We see it especially in the liturgy of the hours, that daily unfolding of prayer that honors the movement of the earth from dawn's first breaking open to the holy crucible of night's stillness. Living our way into these rhythms each day and each year gives us a way of honoring the integrity of our soul's own cycles and rhythms. These rhythms were essential to the desert, Celtic, and Benedictine monks.

Each of the great Celtic harvest festivals happens at the midway points between the solstices and equinoxes. Each festival is considered to be a threshold time when the veil is thin between worlds. I offer here just a brief overview of this cycle of honoring the seasons' unfolding.

Samhain: A Time of Remembrance

November 1 is the midway point between autumn equinox and winter solstice and is the beginning of the new year in Celtic tradition. This feast is called Samhain (pronounced *sow-en*).

It coincides with the Christian celebration of All Saint's Day on November 1 and All Soul's Day on November 2, which begin a whole month that honors those who have died. We tend to neglect our ancestral heritage in American culture, but in other cultures, remembering one's ancestors is an intuitive and essential way of beginning anything new. We benefit from recognizing the tremendous wisdom we can draw upon from those who have traveled the journey before us and whose DNA we carry in every fiber of our bodies.

In the ancient Celtic imagination, this midway point was considered to be an especially "thin time," when the veil between heaven and earth grew more transparent and the wisdom of our ancestors was closer to us. We are reassured that we are not alone, that we share the world with a great "cloud of witnesses" and "communion of saints" just across the veil.

Winter invites us to gather inside, grow still with the landscape, and listen for the voices we may not hear during other times of year. These may be the sounds of our own inner wisdom or the voices of those who came before us. This season call us into the grace of descent. We spend so much of our spiritual lives trying to ascend. Descent is the path of having everything that offered comfort stripped away. In the mystical tradition, the descent is also the slow revelation of the true face and incredible mystery that is God.

Imbolc: A Time of Awakening

Imbolc is the midway point between winter solstice and spring equinox. February 1 and 2 mark a confluence of several feasts and occasions including the Celtic feast of Imbolc, St. Brigid's Day, Candlemas (Feast of the Presentation), and Groundhog Day. In Celtic cultures it is considered to be the very beginning of spring.

As the days slowly lengthen in the northern hemisphere and the sun makes her way higher in the sky, the ground beneath our feet begins to thaw. The earth softens and the seeds deep below stir in the darkness. The word *imbolc* means "in the belly." The earth's belly is beginning to awaken, new life is stirring, seeds are sprouting forth.

In many places the ground is still frozen or covered with snow, but the call now is to tend to those very first signs of movement beneath the fertile ground. What happens when you listen ever so closely in the stillness? What do you hear beginning to emerge?

On the eve of January 31, it is traditional to leave a piece of cloth or ribbon outside the house. It was believed that St. Brigid's spirit traveled across the land and left her curative powers in the *brat Bride* (Brigid's mantle or cloth). It was then used throughout the year as an instrument of healing from sickness and protection from harm.

Beltane: A Time of Flourishing

Beltane, which means "bright fire," is the next cross-quarter day, representing the midpoint between the spring equinox and the summer solstice, and it is often experienced at the height of spring. In Ireland it is considered to be the beginning of summer and the beginning of the light half of the year. We can feel the significant shift in light at this latitude, and the days become significantly longer. Temperatures are warmer. Flowering has come to its fullness. Birds are singing in full chorus.

In Ireland the cuckoo birds start arriving from their winter in Africa, and there are music and walking festivals named after the birds' return. The power of nature's life force coming back is celebrated.

Two fires are lit and the sheep and cattle are brought to the summer pastures. It is a fire festival of fertility and garlands of flowers are made up in honor of the creative abundance beginning to stream forth from the land.

In the pre-Christian tradition, the theme of Beltane is union of male and female energies to increase fertility. Couples would go off into the woods to gather flowers the night before and return with hair and clothes rumpled. Upon their return at dawn, they would scatter flowers on the doorways and windowsills as blessing.

A well-known tradition is the Maypole, with ribbons and streamers and the dancing that occurs around it, a tradition that often ended with a great banquet. The dew of May was thought to hold special properties. Women would bathe in it to renew their complexions. Men would wash their hands in it to increase their skills. Many would walk barefoot in it or roll in the wet grass for healing. In the Catholic Church, the month of May is dedicated to Mary and her fruitfulness.

Lughnasa: The Time of Harvest

Lughnasa (pronounced *loo-nassah*) is an ancient Celtic feast celebrated on August 1, halfway between summer solstice and autumn equinox, marking the time of the beginning of the harvest and the gathering in. It is said to originally honor the Celtic sun god Lugh, who was an ally to the farmer in the struggle for food.

Lughnasa is a time to gather in and to reap what has been sown. It is sometimes thought of as the time of "first fruits" and is when the grain is gathered in. One of the central rituals for this feast is cutting the first corn and making it into a loaf for the Mass at church on August 1 or 2. In the Hebrides in Scotland, it is recorded that families would celebrate Lughnasa on August 15 in connection with the Feast of the Assumption of Mary. Each family member would take a piece of the bread and walk sunwise around the festival fire and sing a song to Mary.

The other liturgical connection is the Feast of the Transfiguration on August 6, tying Lughnasa with the appearance of Christ in glory to Peter, James, and John on the mountain. The apostles are filled with an ecstasy from which they do not want to awaken. In some Christian traditions, the interpretation of the text is that rather than Christ changing, the eyes of the apostles were opened so they could see him in his true form.

Discernment and Sacred Rhythms

The invitation into ripening on our discernment journey means we must be willing to attend to our own nourishment and care until the season is ripe. We must do so not a moment before or after, which is why our loving and mindful attention becomes so important and why we must stay present through the discomfort of it all.

I don't remember exactly when I realized that the earth's cycles were such a profound source of wisdom for me. I think the awareness really deepened for me after my mother died. At the age of 61, she became ill with a life-threatening infection quite suddenly and went into the ICU, where she died five days later. John and I had the incredible privilege of accompanying her across that threshold.

It was the most harrowing time of my life. I was not ready to let go of her. I struggled with depression for a long while following. It was an underworld journey of loss, abandonment, and deep grief.

What sustained me were long walks in Seattle, up the hill our neighborhood was built on, and through Volunteer Park where the trees offered me solace and companionship. My mother died in October, and returning home after her memorial service, I was surrounded by the witness of thousands of jeweled leaves surrendering their hold on the branches and fluttering their way toward earth, where they would become compost for new life. For a few moments I could find some beauty in death.

As autumn gave way to winter, those bare limbs, stretched black against the sky, revealed the essence of trees and the way that death can open us to the essence of life. I was able to see the trees in a different way and came to appreciate the beauty of sparseness.

When the following spring came, I was far from my own blossoming, but I had come to relish the earth's turning as a mirror for my own soul's ripening in ways I hadn't understood before. It would take several years for my heart to heal and for me to reap some of the tremendous gifts that come from being willing to walk through suffering with eyes wide open. I am deeply grateful to my spiritual director and soul friends who offered me solace when needed and firm reminders to offer myself lavish compassion.

What Is It the Season For?

If we move too quickly into the work we feel called to do without the necessary preparation, without the demanding soul work that lays a strong foundation, we actually do ourselves and others harm.

One of the greatest gifts I have found in being a spiritual director, teacher, writer, and supervisor of soul care practitioners is that this path calls me to be very honest with myself. If I am to teach about the value of contemplative ways of being and advocate for radical self-care, I had better begin with myself. I am called each day to renew my commitment to these practices. Often the shadow side of teaching is not making the time or space for the very principles you espouse to others.

Another shadow side is withholding your gifts for fear of not being ready to offer them to the world. We prepare, we practice, we pray, we root ourselves in the Spirit, and then when the season is ripe, we step out into the world with all of its discomfort and offer ourselves with humility and generosity. We may encounter seasons along the way in which we are called again to pull back and strengthen up our interior dwellings. This points again to the essential nature of a soul friend in our lives who can help us discern when we are ready, when we are rushing, and when we are holding back.

Years ago when we lived in Berkeley, I had a wise spiritual director named Clare, and she frequently asked me the question, "What is it the season for?" That simple question is one I return to again and again, to check in and see out of the many things calling for my energy and attention: Which one is it the season for right now?

Living a life of integrity demands this kind of inner commitment. The desert elders were conscious of their role as teachers in the community, even if they never stepped foot in the classroom. They could live their lives as a witness to a different way of being in the world, one which cultivated presence and peace both within and without.

St. Dearbhla

Dearbhla is said to have lived in the sixth century and was of noble lineage in county Meath. Like many women of her time, she was supposed to marry but didn't want to. So she fled to Belmullet in the northwest portion of county Mayo. Her betrothed followed her there, much to her dismay. She asked him why he loved her, and he swooned over her beautiful eyes. The story tells us that she then plucked them out of her head and extended them out to him. He was, of course, horrified, and ran away.

Dearbhla is then said to have washed her eyes in the waters of the holy well and her eyes and sight were miraculously restored. Interestingly, she is not the only woman saint to have disfigured herself to get rid of a suitor; Brigid is said to have made herself look hideous to scare someone away and then was later healed.

Dearbhla set up her monastery at that location, and there is still a church ruin and a well dedicated to her there today. We sadly don't have much more information about her life story, but again, I love that that landscape still holds stones and water dedicated to her memory and the service she offered to her community.

Call upon St. Dearbhla to companion you throughout the seasons and to help illuminate the wisdom found in each one.

Scripture Reflection by John Valters Paintner

Lectio Divina

> For everything there is a season, and a time for every matter under heaven:
>> a time to be born, and a time to die;
>> a time to plant, and a time to pluck up what is planted;

a time to kill, and a time to heal;
a time to break down, and a time to build up;
a time to weep, and a time to laugh;
a time to mourn, and a time to dance;
a time to throw away stones, and a time to gather
    stones together;
a time to embrace, and a time to refrain from
    embracing;
a time to seek, and a time to lose;
a time to keep, and a time to throw away;
a time to tear, and a time to sew;
a time to keep silence, and a time to speak;
a time to love, and a time to hate;
a time for war, and a time for peace.
                                            —Ecclesiastes 3:1–8

Biblical Context

Allegedly, the book of Ecclesiastes is written by Qoheleth, who is King Solomon, someone claiming to be King Solomon (or at least inspired by him), or a pseudonym given by a later editor to give more credence to the book by associating it with someone known for his wisdom. Regardless, the author of the book of Ecclesiastes wrestles with not just what is the meaning of it all but if there is meaning in any of it. All seems to be vanity to Qoheleth, who does oddly acknowledge the importance and joy of work. There are pleasures to be found in life. And yet, even these seem to lack meaning, as they are fleeting.

Like many books of the Bible, this one is written from the place between the profound longing to understand and the deep frustration of not knowing. Like many of us, Qoheleth struggles to understand something that he admits is beyond full human comprehension. And yet, it cannot be ignored.

In this specific passage, familiar to many from the Pete Seeger song made famous by the Byrds, Qoheleth delves into the proper timing for everything. There is, the author argues, an organization to life and the universe. However, it can be difficult for humans to determine when the right time is because it is only God who truly knows.

Personal Reflection

Christine still teases me about how, when I was a classroom teacher in Seattle, I hated snow days because they threw off my lesson plans. (I was very proud that I always had all my units and lesson plans for the entire school year planned out before the first day of classes and so any interruption was not appreciated.) Part of the problem was that, as a native Californian, I somehow never learned to anticipate snow. And even though I now live even further north, I still haven't. The changing of the seasons still manages to take me by surprise.

My first taste of these seasonal transitions was the cherry trees that surrounded our condo building in Seattle. Even though the time between the first bursting bud to the last falling petal was only about a week, I looked forward to those days all year long. I didn't even mind when the beautiful pink petals on the trees became a brown, slippery mess on the pavement. I wasn't saddened when the trees were full of green leaves. I even learned to love seeing the bare branches, because it meant that the pink blossoms would soon return.

I'm not normally a patient person. But if I know how long I have to wait or know that it's only a matter of when and not if, then I'll be fine.

It's no secret that Christine and I are not fans of the phrase "Everything happens for a reason." It's not that we don't believe in cause and effect or divine intervention. It just always comes across as so trite. It sounds like it means more than it's actually saying, which isn't really anything.

And so, to say that everything has its proper time . . . it may be true, but it doesn't really mean anything.

The issue isn't knowing that different things require different timing; it's knowing when that time actually is. That's what the author struggles with here. This passage is more of an acknowledgment of the problem than a solution in and of itself.

What the changing of the seasons continues to teach me is to be present. Complaining about the past won't change it. And worrying about the future won't speed it up. Having to wait for my favorite season has taught me patience and to be in the present season. It has helped me feel grateful for the gifts of each season and understand how they flow one into another. We can't have a new spring without the work of summer and the rest of autumn and winter.

A greater appreciation of where we are can help us anticipate what comes next.

Photography Exploration: Signs of the Season

For this chapter's invitation to a contemplative walk, after you have allowed time to center yourself and open the eyes of your heart, hold this image of ripening and seasonal wisdom as you move through the world. Receive images that express different stages of ripening in whatever season you find yourself in.

When you return home, select two to three images and allow them to speak in their own voice, beginning with "I am . . . ." Step into the image and speak from its perspective. How do you experience the world in this way?

After exploring several images, allow some to enter into a dialogue. Start a new page, and considering one of the images that is speaking strongly to you right now, begin with the question "What is it the season for?" Then free write any response that arises.

Remember there is no "right" way to do this. These are just prompts to get you thinking in different ways and to access the voice of the images.

Writing Exploration: French Pantoum

Those of you who have journeyed through other books or online retreats of mine may already be familiar with this poetic form of the French pantoum. For those of you who are new to it, I love it because it is very accessible and has a wonderful echoing quality that brings images full circle, much like the seasons.

Read through your writing in response to this chapter's reflection questions and the photos. Circle or underline six phrases in your journal that shimmer for you, surprise you, or somehow call out to you.

Once you have chosen the six, begin to enter them below or on a separate piece of paper. You will see that lines one, two, three, four, six, and eight all call for new lines, which are each of the phrases you underlined. Don't try to put them in the "right" order or otherwise manipulate the experience. Then follow the directions for the other lines, which are repetitions of previous lines of the poem.

Once completed, read it through and receive your images in a new way. Consider what title this piece wants to have and what it is revealing to you.

French Pantoum

Stanza 1

Line 1 (new line):_____

Line 2 (new line):_____

Line 3 (new line):_____

Line 4 (new line):_____

Stanza 2

Line 5 (repeat line 2, in stanza 1): _____

Line 6 (new line): _____

Line 7 (repeat line 4, in stanza 1): _____

Line 8 (new line): _____

Stanza 3

Line 9 (repeat line 6): _____

Line 10 (repeat line 3, in stanza 1): _____

Line 11 (repeat line 8): _____

Line 12 (repeat line 1, in stanza 1): _____

Closing Blessing

Seasonal wisdom invites us to consider what is coming to ripeness in our lives right now and how we might respond. I shared the story of Dearbhla discerning her own call to the life of a monk and trying to find any way she can to deter the man pursuing her. I love the absolute trust she offers with her eyes in this story; we can assume it is archetypal rather than literal, but that doesn't make its meaning any less profound. I share a poem I wrote, inspired by her eyes and her trust in the divine.

What does this season of life call forth from you? Where are you aware of still needing to ripen?

st. Dearbhla's eyes

Fleeing from Meath to Mayo
her betrothed gave chase,
she turned to face him, ask
what he loved about her,
"your eyes" came in ardent reply
so she plucked them out
each a perfect orb
cool in her hands like beads
and in horror he fled.

She stood there smiling
surprising even herself
relief rushed down her limbs,
she bent over the well,
splashed her face
and those hollow sockets
with scent of mineral and moss,
sight restored in a flash.

She looked at the world
as if for the first time,

she could finally see
how her God was always
on the side of freedom,
how everything glistens,

and how we must risk everything,
trust we were meant
for this, as if telling
the truth for the first time,

as if our hearts
had been plucked out too
and set ablaze
for all the world to see.[3]

chapter 11

The practice of Landscape as Theophany

We have already seen in our chapters on thresholds and walking the rounds how place is such an important concept in the Celtic imagination. Places can be sacred, and there are specific kinds of places where people have been especially drawn to practice their religion. Places can be called "thin" where we experience the nearness of heaven and earth to each other. There was considered to be a veil between the worlds, and when the veil is thin, we sense the presence of the ancestors and the angels more closely. We encounter the divine in all things.

Physical matter points toward the sacred, so the Incarnation is a living and breathing concept often felt most keenly in creation among trees and mountains, oceans and rivers. Ninth-century Irish theologian John Scotus Eriugena taught that there are indeed two books of revelation—the book of the scriptures and the book of creation. The first is physically small; the second is vast. Both are required to know the fullness of the divine presence. Just as God can speak through the words of the scriptures, so can we hear the voice of the divine in the elements, the creatures, and the land. Therefore the landscape can become a place of theophany, or divine manifestation. The shoreline is a living threshold; the mountain lifts us toward the heavens. The monks sought out places in the wilderness to receive this gift of revelation. The hermitage was a new Eden, a place where the promise of paradise could be tasted in this world.

John O'Donohue described landscape as "the firstborn of creation. It was here hundreds of millions of years before the flowers, the animals, or the people appeared."[1] The land has stories connected to it, and these stories root a people in that particular place. He went on to write that "landscape has a secret and silent memory."[2]

In the book *Celtic Spirituality*, editors Oliver Davies and Thomas O'Loughlin write in their introduction, "In the first place, early Celtic religion appears to have been in the main local, with a particular focus on place. Early Gaulish religion was cultic, centering on specific sacred sites such as woodland glades, lakes, springs, or mountains. The many ancient deposits of weapons and treasure that have been discovered in lakes, rivers, and springs almost certainly reflect a desire to placate or reward a divinity of place."[3]

When we discussed thresholds earlier in this book, we saw how certain points on the landscape such as holy wells emerging from the earth, trees with their roots underground, and mountains were experienced as threshold places where there was access to the otherworld. The editors go on to write of the created world, "both visible and invisible, as a theophany of God."[4]

In the Celtic tradition, creation offers its own form of praise to God. Mary Earle describes it this way: "The sea, the sky, the trees, the animals, the stars—all these are seen to be continually speaking the praise of God, but without human speech. It is the vocation of the whole of creation to praise God, not only in song and poetry, but also in living creatively within the divine design and pattern. We can never exhaust our praise, nor can we ever capture the fullness of God's presence and gift in our prayer."[5] To experience the landscape as a theophany is to take seriously the way the divine can be revealed through nature and through created things. It means we can join in with all of the elements and creatures in singing God's praise.

Landscape, Elements, and Discernment

The elements play a significant role in the Celtic imagination and connect us intimately to the land. Ireland is a place of fierce winds, sacred stones, ritual fires, the power of the sea, and the gift of water in the holy wells. The elements also help connect us to the wisdom of ripening.

The element of wind or air calls us to breathe in more fully. In the west of Ireland where I live, the first winter I resisted the wind. It felt so relentless. The second year I learned to yield to it and discovered how it would strip me free of things I didn't need to hold onto anymore.

Fire reminds us of what we are passionate about and where our sparks need kindling. We don't often see the sun in rain-soaked Ireland, but when it does come out, it is often glistening off wet grass and stone, creating its own kind of brilliance.

Water calls us to follow the flow and not try to force things. Ireland is of course surrounded by the sea, but it is also traversed by rivers and lakes. Holy wells gush forth from the land, offering their blessing.

Earth grounds us and reminds us that we are of the earth and will return to the earth. To the south of us in Galway is the limestone landscape of the Burren, a place where bedrock is exposed and hills push forth. To the west of us is Connemara with its haunting granite mountains covered with bog and heather. I have learned to love stone since living here and letting it teach me about what endures.

St. Enda of Inishmore

St. Enda was originally a warrior king in the province of Ulster. His sister had already become an abbess and tried to convinced him to do likewise. At first, Enda was willing to lay down his arms, but he wanted to marry and asked his sister for a wife from the convent. His sister agreed, but the woman she promised died and she asked her brother to look at the corpse and see the reality that we will all die. He had a change of heart and decided to study for the priesthood.

In the year 484, his brother, who was a king in the province of Munster, gave Enda some land on the island of Inishmore, one of the three Aran islands, where he set up a monastery. Enda is known as "the patriarch of Irish monasticism" because of his impact on the spread of monastic spirituality; most of the monks of his time would have at least visited Enda to gain wisdom from him, including St. Ciaran, St. Brendan, St. Columcille, and St. Sourney. Inishmore became an important pilgrimage destination.

Inishmore is still a very sacred place to spend time. We visit on our pilgrimages for the day and spend six nights when we go on a writing retreat. The island is covered with various holy ruins of ancient churches dedicated to various saints. At the very western end of the island are what is known as the Seven Churches, a site so named because of its size and importance. Seven was a sacred number. On the eastern end of the island is the monastery Enda founded and the place he is said to be buried. On the smallest of the Aran islands, Inisheer, there is also a holy well dedicated to St. Enda.

Call upon St. Enda to help reveal the holiness of landscape to you and to see the world around you with new eyes.

Scripture Reflection by John Valters Paintner

Lectio Divina

> He said, "Go out and stand on the mountain before the LORD, for the LORD is about to pass by." Now there was a great wind, so strong that it was splitting mountains and breaking rocks in pieces before the LORD, but the LORD was not in the wind; and after the wind an earthquake, but the LORD was not in the earthquake; and after the earthquake a fire, but the LORD was not in the fire; and after the fire a sound of sheer silence. When Elijah heard it, he wrapped his face in his mantle and went out and stood at the entrance of the cave.
> —1 Kings 19:11–13

Biblical Context

Most of the individuals we think of as "the prophets," that is, those with books of the Bible named after them, were actually just the spokesmen of a larger prophetic movement. They were the frontmen, if you would, of a group or school of people with a similar goal or message.

Elijah is the rare exception to this. He was a lone prophet. Elijah did start off as a member of a group of prophets whose focus was preaching against King Ahab and Queen Jezebel. Individually, each of these rulers were horrible. They cared nothing for God and routinely abused their power over the Israelites. Perhaps worst of all, they egged each other on to greater heights of evil cruelty. So when Elijah and his brethren preached against Ahab and Jezebel, undermining their authority among the people, the king and queen took it as a personal affront for which they would seek revenge. Unfortunately, only Elijah survived the culling of the prophets.

Elijah ran away to hide for a time, finding shelter with a widow and her son, but he eventually returned in a big way. In chapter 18, Elijah challenged the four hundred and fifty priests of Ba'al to a duel, of sorts. Tired of the people wavering back and forth between God and the false idols of Jezebel, Elijah hoped to publically and dramatically remind the Israelites, once and for all, who they should be following.

Elijah and the priests of Ba'al both built wooden altars to their respective deities and prayed for the altar to be set alight through divine action. Elijah allowed the other side to go first, verbally taunting the numerous priest of Ba'al, going so far as to suggest that Ba'al might be away or taking a nap. When it was Elijah's turn, he doused his altar in water to make things more difficult. But God answered Elijah's prayer. His altar burned bright, and the people recommitted themselves to the Lord and the covenant, having been shown the power of God.

Unfortunately, this triumph was short-lived. The Israelites may have returned to the covenant, but Queen Jezebel was furious when she learned that her priests were defeated. Elijah, once again, had to flee for his life.

Elijah escaped into the wilderness, where he soon became exhausted and collapsed. He prayed for death, both physically and spiritually drained. Only the intervention of an angel with food and drink could encourage Elijah on further.

When the last prophet reached a cave in the holy Mount Horeb, God confronted Elijah, asking him why he was there. Elijah quickly recounted all that he had done and that the king and queen were now seeking to take his life. God told Elijah to wait outside for God to pass.

While Elijah waited, a great and mighty wind swept across the mountain, crushing rocks. But God was not in the wind. Next an earthquake struck the mountain, but God was not in the earthquake. After the earthquake a fire raged across the mountain, but again God was not in the fire. Only after the wind and the earthquake and the fire was there a tiny whispering sound. And God was in the tiny whispering sound.

Elijah was so overcome with the presence of God that he hid his face in his hands.

Personal Reflection

How very human of Elijah to go from the thrill of victory to the agony of defeat in what seems like an instant. One moment, Elijah and the Israelites are celebrating God's victory over the false idols of the wicked queen. The next, there is a price on his head and he's on the run . . . again.

In modern society, when someone goes away to the wilderness to "get away from it all," it's more a metaphor than anything else. For Elijah, it was quite literal. Jezebel, being a vengeful person, wanted Elijah dead and she had the resources to make that happen. The last prophet of the Lord was so distraught that even though he got away, he still wanted to end his life. He couldn't take the pressure of being pursued and persecuted, again. Elijah even comes across as a bit manic, ecstatic one moment and praying for death the next. It was feast or famine for him, with very little in between.

Fortunately for Elijah, and us, he found the comfort and aide he needed out in nature.

Most people know Mount Sinai as the place where Moses receives the Ten Commandments. But another retelling of that account places Moses on Mount Horeb. It's the same mountain range, just a different peak. Such high places were often seen as sacred places for the Israelites and other ancient peoples. The encounter between Elijah and his rivals, the priests of Ba'al, took place on Mount Carmel.

And so it's very interesting to note that in this very important passage, God is not actually found in what traditional insurance policies might categorize as "acts of God." Elijah did not encounter God in the mighty wind. The wind shook the mountain and crushed boulders, but no God there. Elijah didn't find God in the earthquake, either. Again, an entire mountain range is being tossed about and no God. Even when a destructive fire rages over the land, consuming everything in its path, Elijah did not find God.

But were those three natural disasters necessary for Elijah to appreciate the silence that followed? Maybe Elijah needed to have his expectations disappointed before he could see past them to see something new. If we are so laser-focused on looking for what we expect, we can miss the obvious.

Besides, the tiny whispering wind that comes last, the thing in which Elijah encounters God, is just as natural as the three big events that preceded it. If Elijah only looked for God in the grandiose, he would have missed God in the subtle and the delicate. A gentle, babbling brook is just as much a part of Creation as the mighty, crashing waves of the ocean.

The Practice of Sacred Landcape

One of the things that draws so many people today to the Celtic Christian tradition is its sense of intimacy with the earth and creation as a place of *theophany*, meaning "appearance of God." For ancient monks, nature was one of the two sacred texts of revelation, alongside the scriptures. They reverenced and honored both.

The Celtic monks saw that all of creation offers praise to God, as Psalm 104 describes. The great and powerful sea, the wide sky, the creatures, the sacred trees, and the force of wind and rain are all seen as participating in a liturgy of praise, which our own worship joins.

St. Columbanus said, "Understand, if you want to know the Creator, know created things." If we want to come to know God, we must grow intimate with God's artistry. Nature reveals the divine in unique ways. Her rhythms and ways offer insight into God's rhythms and ways.

When we awaken to the holy shimmering in each flower, tree, and bird, we suddenly discover that we are woven into a vast community. We find ourselves nourished and supported in ways we didn't see before. We are called to hold this deepening awareness and trust that our own holy birthing is sustained and called forth by the choirs of creation.

Make a commitment in the coming days to spend time in nature and be present to it as theophany, that is, as a place of revelation. Bring the prayers of your heart and ask for signs and symbols to guide you on the way.

Photography Exploration: Features of the Landscape

Make some time to go for another contemplative walk. This time attune your eyes to the features of the landscape where you live. This might be urban or rural, mountainous or coastal, plains or rivers. When you think of where you live, what aspect of the landscape shimmers most strongly for you? Is there a particular mountain or lake, a beach or even a skyscraper that evokes a sense of awe for you?

Visit this place and spend some time there with your camera. Receive images of the land and see what you notice when you look with the eyes of your heart. How does the landscape where you live shape your own inner journey? What does the land invite you to consider in your discernment process?

Writing Exploration: Poem of Instruction

You are invited to write a poem of instruction. This poetry form essentially instructs someone how to do something. Consider the journey you have made so far through this material and what wisdom you have to offer. What would you write to yourself just a few weeks ago? Or as a reminder to yourself for the weeks ahead? Or to someone else struggling with discernment? The title of the poem could be "How to Discern" or "How to Be a Pilgrim" or "How to Seek" or anything that calls to you at this point in the journey.

Closing Blessing

Inishmore is a very holy place and one I never get tired of visiting. I love when we get to spend several nights there and sink into the silence of the place. I wrote a poem imagining Enda first arriving to this island and what might have shimmered for him and called him to stay.

What landscapes call most strongly to you? Where do you feel most at home?

st. Enda Arrives on Inishmore

It must have been the light
slanting across veils of rain,
when this island, all grey stone and bare
became a vision in gold and gleam

or perhaps it was the smell of sea,
wind swirling up the stony spine,
gulls criss-cross, weaving a new story,
one more truly your own

and something in you had already
bowed low, astonished,
you found yourself singing
after so many years of silence

and the great betrayals of your life
sheared away like winter's wool,
a quiet descends on your thoughts
and you know there is no leaving.

Slowly, hundreds follow also seeking
the way light and water and stone
can remind of elemental things,
how time suspends as it travels

out on the tide,
returns with its offering:
your reflection in the pools formed
on shore, you no longer look through but in.

chapter 12

The practice of Three Essential Things

Three is a sacred number in the Celtic tradition and often the saints were said to have expressed their own desires or commitments in terms of the number three. St. Columcille of Iona asked God for three things—virginity, wisdom, and pilgrimage[1]—while St. Ita of Killeedy is said to have focused on faith, simplicity, and generosity.[2]

The desert monks also loved to gather principles to live by in threes; here are two of their sayings around this:

> Abba Andrew said, "These three things are appropriate for a monk: exile, poverty, and endurance in silence." (Andrew 1)[3]

> As he was dying, Abba Benjamin said to his sons, "If you observe the following, you can be saved, Be joyful at all times, pray without ceasing, and give thanks for all things." (Benjamin 4)[4]

Each is a variation on the three essential things one must do in life. I love that they come in threes as three is a number which helps us break past dualities. We tend to view life in either/or, black/white dichotomies. When the third possibility enters we are invited to hold the complexity and mystery of life and realize that life is so much vaster. Franciscan priest Richard Rohr, O.F.M., describes this as the "third eye" of the mystics which moves us into non-dualistic thinking. Three is, of course, also the number of the Trinity.

Esther de Waal points out that "traditionally the Celtic people with their love of formulating things and their passion for significant numbers have always given special veneration to the number three. Most beloved of all was the triad, an arrangement of three statements that summed up a thing or person or quality or mood, or simply linked otherwise incompatible things."[5]

None of the monks say the same three things. Does this mean that one is right and the others are wrong? Or does it open us up to the possibility that the ground can shift beneath us during our lives and what feels essential during one season becomes of less importance in another?

What I love about the desert elders and Celtic monks is that they do not offer a systematic, ten-step program for living a life in God. Each monk speaks from his or her own experience, each offers the wisdom earned from years of practice. Their stories point to the need to stay committed to one's own truth in this moment with the guidance of wise elders and to see past the dualisms we worship.

Discerning What Is Essential

These stories also remind us again that each saying was spoken from a wise elder in response to the specific life concern for a disciple in that moment of their lives. We may be tempted to want to have a list of the three essential things we must do for wholeness or freedom. What we discover is that this might shift during our lives. What worked for one season might need to change focus in another. This also reminds us of the importance of having a wise elder or soul friend in our lives who can help us to discern what the essential things are in our life right now.

Awareness of our own mortality can have a significant impact on what we come to believe is most essential. As we come toward the end of this book, I offer a rather stark note, because this was such an important part of the monastic way, to "keep death daily before your eyes," as St. Benedict wrote in his Rule. It is perhaps all the more essential when we are in a season of discerning what our deepest life loves are, to remember that our time here is not endless and there is a sense of urgency about letting go of the things that stand in the way of our saying yes to the truest part of ourselves.

We live in a culture very disconnected from the reality of death, especially our own. We constantly seek ways to stave off aging and mortality. We are marketed endless products to keep us young and vital. We deny our grieving hearts in a rush to move on to something more cheerful. This all comes at great cost to the well-being of our souls.

Being mindful of eventual death need not be morbid, but calls us to always return to that which is essential. Spiritual writer Alan Jones describes the desert relationship to death in this way: "Facing death gives our loving force, clarity, and focus . . . even our despair is to be given up and seen as the ego-grasping device that it really is. Despair about ourselves and our world is, perhaps, the ego's last and, therefore, greatest attachment."[6]

In the desert and Celtic traditions, death is a friend and companion along the journey, assisting us in releasing everything that is not God. Keeping death before us was never meant to be a morbid preoccupation but a profound honoring of the way our mortality can bring us so close to the essential things of life.

The year I turned forty, I had a pulmonary embolism which brought me much closer to the reality of my own eventual death than I ever wanted to experience, and yet it also brought luminosity to my world. I cherished my life as I never had before. I continue to know the closeness of that reality, and it fosters gratitude for each moment.

What if each morning you awoke with a sense of life's incredible gift, to be alive for another day, to have another opportunity to love again? How might that break open your discernment in new ways? What commitments would fall away as no longer necessary?

This is a time to consider the fact that each of us will one day be asked to relinquish our most precious possession, our very lives. And that reality asks us to make a choice between living in fear and anxiety and living in an overwhelming sense of gratitude. Sister Death can become a graced companion when she is called upon daily as a portal into deepened cherishing of living.

St. Ita and the Three Stones

Ita was a sixth-century Irish saint and is the second most significant woman saint in Ireland after Brigid. Her hagiographer even called her a "second Brigid," and her name, Ita, means "thirst." She established a church in Limerick called Killeedy, which means "church of Ita."

When Ita was young, she received a dream in which she was gifted three precious stones. She was unsure as to its meaning and pondered it. Later, in another visitation, it was revealed to her that throughout her life she would receive many dreams and visions, and the three stones represented the gifts of the Trinity coming to her. I love this affirmation of the multitude that God is as well.

When she was older, Ita prayed for a place to found her monastery and was again shown her direction in a dream. She was told to leave her native land and come to a new place at the foot of a hill.

At the monastery Ita founded, many young people were sent her way for education and she became a teacher to St. Brendan, who would later go on his great voyage. She told her students to follow the "Rule of the Saints of Ireland" because she felt strongly about the Celtic value of soul friends and saw those across the veil as guides as well.

St. Brendan once asked Ita what were the three things most pleasing and displeasing to God. She replied that what pleased God were "true faith in God with a pure heart, a simple life with a grateful spirit, and generosity inspired by charity." What was most displeasing were "a mouth that hates people, a heart harboring resentments, and confidence in wealth."[7]

Call upon St. Ita to help you discern what the three essential things in this season of your life are.

Scripture Reflection by John Valters Paintner

Lectio Divina

> He has told you, O mortal, what is good;
> and what does the LORD require of you
> but to do justice, and to love kindness,
> and to walk humbly with your God?
> —Micah 6:8

Biblical Context

The prophet Micah was a contemporary of First Isaiah (Isaiah of Jerusalem was successful enough to head a movement that outlasted him and spawned two later disciples who added to his book in his name). Even though both men wrote about beating "swords into plowshares and spears into pruning hooks" (Is 2:4 and Mi 4:3), it's unlikely that Isaiah, a well-educated and politically connected priest from the capital, and Micah, a simple country boy, socialized with one another. However, the latter does get mention in the book of Jeremiah in reference to King Hezekiah's religious reforms.

Isaiah's lengthy book covers both matters of fidelity to the covenant and justice toward the Chosen People. Micah's much shorter book of prophesy focuses on the sinful corruption of those in the capital cities of Jerusalem and Samaria. His concise writing has a beauty of efficiency that doesn't often get the credit it deserves.

Like most prophets, Micah used what modern scholars refer to as a "speech of judgment." It's a clever combination of a legal framework layered with poetic imagery. As the covenant was seen as a type of legal contract between God and the people, a sin (whether it be personal or communal) occurred when the Law of God (the Ten Commandments) was broken. This speech of judgment was a way of calling the people to task. It would start with a call to attention, for the people to "hear" or to "listen" to the words of the prophet.

This would be followed by a list of witnesses, anything from the people themselves to the nations or even creation. Then the prophets would get down to the business of naming names and handing down indictments—that is, what the people named had done wrong. The prophet then would end with a poetic exploration of what would happen to the accused should they continue their misconduct. (Individual prophets varied in both style and whether they wanted the punishments to actually happen or if they hoped to scare the accused into repentance—a few were even a bit upset when the punishment didn't happen or didn't happen soon enough for their liking.)

In chapter 6 of his book, Micah began with a call to the mountains and hills to bear witness to his words. Through a series of rhetorical questions, the prophet laid out the reason why the people should be following the covenant wholeheartedly: they would still be slaves in Egypt if God hadn't rescued their ancestors. (Notice that there is no attempt to bribe the people with a promise of eternal life if they are faithful. God has already graced them with their lives and the Promised Land.) What Micah accused the people of is hollow rituals, of going through the motions without truly understanding what the covenant is. It was not enough that they sacrificed animals or recited prayers, particularly if they were mistreating the poor and vulnerable. Their punishment was clear. Their behavior would lead to the land no longer being bountiful and it being taken from them by other nations.

But in the midst of this condemnation by Micah, the prophet laid out a remedy to their predicament. He didn't just tell them what they were doing wrong; he told them what they should be doing. Micah offered his own three essential things for the people to follow: to do justice, to love kindness, and to walk humbly with their God.

Personal Reflection

If you're thinking, "That's easier said than done," I'd agree. There's a reason that even as the people are ticking all the right boxes (performing the right rituals and saying the correct prayers), they've still got it all wrong.

Micah's three-step answer is, at best, vague and elicits more questions than tangible action plans.

It reminds me of when, as a young college student, I returned from World Youth Day. It was my first trip to Europe, and I was enjoying time with my church friends when the unexpected happened: I had a spiritual awakening at an international religious conference. The words of Pope John Paul II challenging the youth of the world to not be afraid of being holy moved me in a way I hadn't expected. (Did I mention I was young?)

I returned to the States truly on fire for my reclaimed faith. I was determined to not be afraid to be holy. Only . . . what does "being holy" mean? How does one do "holy"?

I eventually found my way, but for a few months there I was equally confused and frustrated.

In the time of Micah, the people were not willing to listen to his words of warning and advice, but for those living during the Exile and us today, what precisely is he suggesting? The blessing and the curse here is that while not completely subjective, his call is very personal. We must all work out what this means for us.

How does one "do justice"? Well, according to scripture, this one's fairly easy. The Bible is full of commandments and examples of God playing favorites. That's right; God has a weak spot for widows, orphans, the poor, the oppressed, the foreigner, the outcast, and others in difficult situations. To "do justice" in the eyes of God means to care first and foremost for those who struggle to care for themselves due to the inequities of society. There's a reason the prophets emerged during times of great economic inequality. It is not an easy task to work for justice in an age of greed and fear. Even when I am very intentional about this, it is a challenge to feel as though I'm making a difference. But that doesn't let me off the hook from trying.

What does it mean to "love kindness"? To truly love something means to put it first, before one's self. So, kindness must be one's first response to people and situations. I know I struggle with this greatly. I wish I were more like my mother than my father in this regard. Kindness doesn't always come easy to me. Yet I recognize its value and so strive to be kinder than I have been in the past. Improvement, not unobtainable perfection, is my goal.

What does "walking humbly with your God" look like? When I imagine this in my mind's eye, I picture myself walking behind God. Or to put it another way: God is before me, first. (Yes, there's a recurring theme here.) It's not to say that everything that follows is unimportant, just that there is a sense of priorities.

I'm not sure if my interpretation of these three essential things (according to the prophet Micah) makes sense to you. I still struggle with this myself. But as I mentioned before, the blessing of this is that you are free to interpret them for yourself. What are *your* three essential things and what do they mean to *you*?

Three Essential Practices

One way to approach the end of this book is to reflect back on the spiritual practices you have engaged in: thresholds, dream work, seeking the place of your resurrection, blessing each moment, soul friends, encircling, walking the rounds, learning by heart, solitude and silence, seasonal cycles, and landscape as theophany. You might consider which three of these practices are ones you feel bring your heart and soul most alive. What is the commitment you want to make going forward? How will you allow this time of practice to shape your days to come?

Consider also reflecting on the three practices or principles in your own life that you count as most essential. Hold them as touchstones for your life right now as you continue to discern what is ripening. I invite you to also enter into this meditation of reflecting on your life from the perspective of your death. For what three kings do you want to be remembered? It is unlikely to be academic degrees, awards, or promotions at work. Allow some time for this to arise of its own accord, no need to force.

Photography Exploration: Three Photos

I invite you for this final chapter to spend some time looking through the photos you have received while making this journey through Celtic practices. As you review them, notice if there are any images that especially shimmer for you or catch your attention in some way. Choose three of those to work with.

Number them 1, 2, and 3. Take some time to journal for a few minutes about each photo: What does it evoke in you? What invitation do you feel arising from it? What does it call you to consider or pay attention to? For this exploration, I want you to really allow some time to let each image speak to your heart.

After this time of writing, go back to the three questions you were invited to write at the very beginning of this book. Match the questions you numbered with the photos and then see how what you just wrote for each image responds to the question you asked when we began. This may require some intuitive leaps. You may find some synchronicities or further food for reflection.

Writing Exploration: Elegy

Inspired by your reflections on your death and how you want to be remembered, I invite you to write your poem this chapter in the form of an elegy.

This does not have to be a morbid exercise, but one in which you celebrate the life you are living and will live before you die. Let this elegy offer joyful praise for the gift of you in this world.

In poetic form, celebrate what you have done for the world. In what ways will you be remembered? What did you build, create, or teach? How has your life impacted others? How have those around you been changed by your presence?

Remember, you are writing this as an imaginative exercise in retrospect. See what images arise.

Closing Blessing

Ultimately, I think what we each seek is transformation. To be transformed means to let go of our control for a while in the hope that something even greater will be revealed in us. When we open ourselves to transformation, we yield our certainties about the world for a new way of seeing.

In the monastic tradition, conversion has always been an important principle. Not conversion as a onetime event to join a religion, but conversion as a continual turning around, a journey of always allowing ourselves to be surprised by God.

Have you discovered your heart opening and receiving? Or is there still resistance, closing off, defensiveness, a thousand reasons why you could never say yes? Be gentle with yourself. Transformation is a slow journey; in fact, conversion teaches us that it is the journey of a lifetime. We are never done. We continue to unfold and grow and stretch and change.

This poem is inspired by the story of Ita's three stones. As you read it, consider: What have you endured, treasured, sparked? What have you hidden away and made visible? What will you carry forth with you?

Dreaming of Stones

In the world before waking
I meet a winged one,
feathered, untethered,
who presses in my palm
three precious stones,
like St. Ita in her dream,
but similarities end there,
her with saintliness and certainty,
me asking questions in the dark.

All I know is
I am not crafted from
patience of rock or gravity of earth,
nor flow of river,
I am not otter with
her hours devoted to play.

I am none of these.
At least not yet.

The stones will still be singing
centuries from now,
made smooth by
all kinds of weather.
If I strike them together,
they spark and kindle.
Do I store them as treasures
to secretly admire
on storm-soaked days?
Or wear them as an amulet
around my neck?

When the angel returns to me
in the harsh truth of last morning,
will she ask
what have I endured,
treasured, and sparked?
Will she ask what have I hidden away
and what made visible?[8]

conclusion

This book has called us to the wild edges, both of the land of Ireland and those wild edges found within each of us. Being on the wild edges is often unsettling. How do we keep from feeling pulled apart? What do we do with the feeling of being moved in too many directions?

What keeps us centered in the midst of this journey of a lifetime is our commitment to practice. When we say yes to becoming more truly ourselves, we are saying yes to a set of ancient practices that will nourish and sustain us. The monks of the desert and of the Celtic lands knew these struggles and longings as well. We say yes to sitting in silence each day and honoring thresholds. We transform our relationship to time by bringing ourselves more fully present to each moment, so suddenly moments of eternity keep breaking through rather than the maddening rush toward the next deadline.

We make time to be nourished by creation and deepen our intimacy with this book of God's revelation. We honor the natural rhythms of creation and our own bodies. We actively cultivate kindred souls to support us on the journey and offer us wisdom. We listen to the night wisdom our dreams can bring. We bring a heart of gratitude each day for the tasks that are our form of expression in the world and send forth blessings. We make time for creative pursuits—writing, painting, dancing, singing, and whatever else brings our hearts joy, trusting that when we deepen into our joy, we deepen into what we were called here to do. We learn words by heart that will nourish us deeply. We practice listening deeply and discerning between what is most life-giving and what drains our energy away. We learn to say no to that which does not truly nurture us.

If you have come to the end of this book expecting a huge revelation about your life purpose, but you are still wondering what that might be, take heart. Remember this is a journey, and sometimes our deepest purpose is discovered in living our ordinary lives with great reverence and attention. Your call may not be to change anything in your life other than your perspective.

This is not a linear journey, and no answers are promised. What is promised is that if you continue to honor the spiral path and allow your soul its own slow time to ripen and unfold, what emerges will be all the richer and less forced, less calculated, less planned out.

I want to offer a deep bow of gratitude to these spiritual ancestors, the desert and Celtic monks and mystics, who lived with courage, clarity, and compassion. Consider continuing to welcome in their wisdom each day of the coming season ahead.

Where are your own invitations to move further onto the wild edge? What are the practices to which you are feeling called to integrate or recommit yourself?

acknowledgments

My gratitude goes primarily to the gorgeous country of Ireland that welcomed us with such open arms five years ago when we came as strangers to live. The warmth of her people and the beauty of her landscape helped us to fall in love long ago and feel like we had come home. Thanks also goes to the hundreds of pilgrims we have now guided here in Ireland, whose own sense of wonder and enthusiasm helped to deepen our love for this place. Finally, gratitude goes to our community of local hosts, guides, artists, and musicians who enrich our experience here and that of our groups immeasurably with their gifts, stories, insights, and craic.

Thanks as well to my dear friends who support me in the creative process and especially to John. I am also always grateful for the great folks at Ave Maria Press who continue to make publishing a pleasure and especially to Amber Elder, who shepherded the editing process with such care.

Appendix I

contemplative photography and lectio Divina

Contemplative Photography

Visio divina (sacred seeing) is a way of seeing the world with the eyes of the heart, which is the place of receptivity and openness, rather than with the mind, which is often the place of grasping and planning. It is an adaptation of the ancient practice of *lectio divina* (sacred reading).

One of the best ways to practice is to go on a contemplative walk, which is a walk where your sole focus is on being present to each moment's invitation as it unfolds, rather than setting out with a particular goal. There is nowhere to "get to." You begin by breathing deeply and centering yourself, bringing your awareness down to your heart center.

Go out in the world for a walk; it could be just down your block or in a nearby park. Bring a camera—a simple camera on your phone is fine. As you walk, stay present to the world as a sacred text, much like you would in lectio divina with the scriptures. Below is a suggested process to move through.

Settling and Shimmering

Breathe deeply. Move your awareness down to your heart center. Settle into this moment. Release any thoughts or expectations. See if you can keep a soft gaze that is diffuse and open, as opposed to a hard stare when you are looking for something.

As you begin walking, pay attention to things around you that shimmer, which means something that calls for your attention, invites you to spend some time with it. It might be a natural object like a tree or branch; it might be a sign in a shop window that catches your attention, or the way light is flooding the street. Stay open to all possibilities for how the world might speak to your heart.

Savoring and Stirring

Stay with what shimmers and allow it to unfold in your heart, savoring your experience.

Make space within for images, feelings, and memories to stir. How does your body respond? What is happening inside in response to this experience?

Summoning and Serving

Slowly shift your awareness to a sense of invitation or summoning that rises up from your prayer. How does the prayer stirring in you meet you in this particular moment of your life? How might you be called into a new awareness or kind of service through this experience?

You might explore with your camera how gazing at this shimmering moment through the lens supports you in seeing it more deeply. The practice of contemplative photography is to "receive images as gifts" rather than to "take photos." If you notice yourself grasping, put the camera down. But if the lens is helping you to see this moment from different perspectives and deepen into it, the camera can be a great gift.

Slowing and Stilling

Once your walk feels complete, return home, release all of the words and images, and slow down even more deeply. Allow yourself some time for silence and stillness. Breathe gratitude in and out. Simply notice your experience.

The Practice of Lectio Divina

First Movement—Lectio: Settling and Shimmering

Begin by finding a comfortable position where you can remain alert and yet also relax your body. Bring your attention to your breath and allow a few moments to become centered. If you find yourself distracted at any time, gently return to the rhythm of your breath as an anchor for your awareness. Allow yourself to settle into this moment and become fully present.

Read your selected scripture passage once or twice through, slowly, and listen for a word or phrase that feels significant right now, capturing your attention even if you don't know why. Gently repeat this word to yourself in the silence.

Second Movement—Meditatio: Savoring and Stirring

Read the text again and then allow the word or phrase which caught your attention in the first movement to spark your imagination. Savor the word or phrase with all of your senses, notice what smells, sounds, tastes, sights, and feelings are evoked. Then listen for what images, feelings, and memories are stirring, welcoming them in, and then savoring and resting into this experience.

Third Movement—Oratio: Summoning and Serving

Read the text a third time and then listen for an invitation rising up from your experience of prayer so far. Considering the word or phrase and what it has evoked for you in memory, image, or feeling, what is the invitation? This invitation may be a summons toward a new awareness or action.

Fourth Movement—Contemplatio: Slowing and Stilling

Move into a time for simply resting in God and allowing your heart to fill with gratitude for God's presence in this time of prayer. Slow your thoughts and reflections even further and sink into the experience of stillness. Rest in the presence of God and allow yourself to simply be. Rest here for several minutes. Return to your breath if you find yourself distracted.

Closing

Gently connect with your breath again and slowly bring your awareness back to the room, moving from inner experience to outer experience. Give yourself some time of transition between these moments of contemplative depth and your everyday life. Consider taking a few minutes to journal about what you experienced in your prayer.[1]

Appendix 2

Resources in Celtic Christian Spirituality

Davies, Oliver, and John O'Laughlin. *Celtic Spirituality.* Mahwah, NJ: Paulist Press, 2000.

de Waal, Esther. *The Celtic Way of Prayer: The Recovery of the Religious Imagination.* New York: Image, 1999.

———. *Every Earthly Blessing: Rediscovering the Celtic Tradition.* Harrisburg, PA: Morehouse Publishing, 1999.

Earle, Mary. *Celtic Christian Spirituality: Essential Writings—Annotated and Explained.* Woodstock, VT: SkyLight Paths, 2011.

———. *Holy Companions: Spiritual Practices from the Celtic Saints.* Harrisburg, PA: Morehouse Publishing, 2004.

Newell, John Philip. *Christ of the Celts: The Healing of Creation.* San Francisco, CA: Jossey-Bass, 2008.

O'Donohue, John. *Anam Ċara: A Book of Celtic Wisdom.* New York: HarperCollins, 1998.

Sellner, Edward C. *Wisdom of the Celtic Saints.* Notre Dame, IN: Ave Maria Press, 1993.

Sheldrake, Philip. *Living between Worlds: Place and Journey in Celtic Spirituality.* Cambridge, MA: Cowley Publications, 1995.

Waddell, Helen. *Beasts and Saints.* Grand Rapids, MI: Eerdmans Publishing, 1996.

Weis, Monica. *Thomas Merton and the Celts: A New World Opening Up*. Eugene, OR: Pickwick Publications, 2016.

Notes

Introduction

1. Oliver Davies and Thomas O'Loughlin, *Celtic Spirituality* (Mahwah, NJ: Paulist Press, 2000), 10–11, Kindle.

2. I share more of the details of this story in my previous book *The Soul of a Pilgrim: Eight Practices for the Journey Within* (Notre Dame, IN: Ave Maria Press, 2015).

3. John O'Donohue, *Anam Ċara: A Book of Celtic Wisdom* (New York: HarperCollins, 1998), 41–42.

4. For a rich resource exploring these three strands, see Benedictine monk Seán Ó'Duinn's book *Where Three Streams Meet: Celtic Spirituality* (Dublin: Columba Press, 2000).

5. Davies and O' Loughlin, *Celtic Spirituality*, 11–12.

6. Timothy Joyce, *Celtic Christianity* (Maryknoll, NY: Orbis, 1998), 36–37.

7. Benedicta Ward, S.L.G., trans., "Abraham 3," in *The Sayings of the Desert Fathers* (Kalamazoo, MI: Cistercian Publications, 1984), 34.

1. The Practice of Thresholds

1. Philip Sheldrake, *Living between Worlds: Place and Journey in Celtic Spirituality* (Cambridge, MA: Cowley Publications, 1995), 30.

2. Michael W. Herren and Shirley Ann Brown, *Christ in Celtic Christianity: Britain and Ireland from the Fifth to the Tenth Century* (Woodbridge, Suffolk: Boydell Press, 2002), 49.

3. Ward, *Sayings of the Desert Fathers*, 4.

4. Dolores Whelan, *Ever Ancient Ever New: Celtic Spirituality in the 21st Century* (Dublin: Columba, 2007), 24.

5. Christine Valters Paintner, "St. Brigid and the Fruit Tree," in *Illuminating the Way: Embracing the Wisdom of Monks and Mystics* (Notre Dame, IN: Ave Maria Press, 2016), 95–96.

3. The Practice of *Peregrinatio* and Seeking Your Place of Resurrection

1. Nora Chadwick, *Age of the Saints in the Early Celtic Church* (London: Oxford University Press, 1961), 64.

2. Sheldrake, *Living between Worlds*, 8.

3. Antonio Machado, from "Proverbios y cantares XXIX" in *Fields of Castile* (Mineola, NY: Dover Publications, 2007), 138–139.

4. Ward, "Poemen 80," in *Sayings of the Desert Fathers*, 178.

5. Ward, "Nisterus 5," in *Sayings of the Desert Fathers*, 155.

6. Paintner, "Flagstone of Loneliness," originally published in *Boyne Berries* 21 (Spring 2017): 39.

4. The Practice of Blessing Each Moment

1. Esther de Waal, *The Celtic Way of Prayer: The Recovery of the Religious Imagination* (New York: Image, 1999), 74–75, Kindle.

2. Benedict, *The Rule of Saint Benedict*, Prologue 8–11.

3. Whitley Stokes, D.C.L., ed., *Lives of Saints from the Book of Lismore* (Oxford, UK: Clarendon Press, 1890), 186–187.

4. Paintner, "St. Gobnait and the Place of Her Resurrection," originally published on *HeadStuff,* https://www.headstuff.org/literature/poem-week-st-gobnait-place-resurrection.

5. The Practice of Soul Friendship

1. Edward Sellner, *Stories of the Celtic Soul Friends* (New York: Paulist Press, 2004), 7.

2. O'Donohue, *Anam Ċara, xviii*.

3. De Waal, *The Celtic Way of Prayer*, 137.

4. Alan Jones, *Soul Making: The Desert Way of Spirituality* (San Francisco: HarperOne, 1989), 101.

5. David Whyte, "The Sun," in *House of Belonging* (Langley, WA: Many Rivers Press, 1997), 90.

6. Esther De Waal, *Every Earthly Blessing: Rediscovering the Celtic Tradition* (Harrisburg, PA: Morehouse, 1999), loc. 1260–1261, Kindle.

7. De Waal, *Every Earthly Blessing*, loc. 1272.

8. David Whyte, "Self-Portrait," in *Fire in the Earth* (Langley, WA: Many Rivers Press, 1992).

9. Paintner, "St. Kevin Holds Open His Hand," originally published in *Skylight* 47, no. 10 (May 2018).

6. The Practice of Encircling

1. Mary C. Earle, *Celtic Christian Spirituality: Essential Writings—Annotated and Explained* (Woodstock, VT: SkyLight Paths, 2011), loc. 264–271, Kindle.

2. This poem is translated from old Irish by Kuno Meyer and is widely available online.

3. De Waal, *The Celtic Way of Prayer*, 156.

4. Sheldrake, *Living between Worlds*, 38.

5. Mary DeJong, "Rewilding Prayer: How Caim Invites Protection for All of Creation," *Waymarkers Journal*, https://www.waymarkers.net/blog/2017/09/14/rewilding-prayer-how-caim-invites-protection-for-all-of-creation.

6. Paintner, "Holy Mountain," originally published on *Galway Review*, https://thegalwayreview.com/2016/02/12/christine-valters-paintner-two-poems.

7. The Practice of Walking the Rounds

1. Joseph Campbell, as quoted in Diane K. Osbon, ed., *Reflections on the Art of Living: A Joseph Campbell Companion* (New York: HarperCollins, 1991), 199.

2. O'Donohue, *Anam Ċara*, 57.

3. Wallace Stevens, *Notes toward a Supreme Fiction* (Omaha, NE: The Cummington Press, 1942), vii.

8. The Practice of Learning by Heart

1. Davies and O'Loughlin, *Celtic Spirituality*, 14.

2. Peter O'Dwyer, *Towards a History of Irish Spirituality* (Dublin: Columba Press, 1995), 50.

3. O'Donohue, *Anam Ċara*, 178.

4. Paintner, "St. Brendan and the Songbirds," in *Illuminating the Way: Embracing the Wisdom of Monks and Mystics* (Notre Dame, IN: Ave Maria Press, 2016), 111.

9. The Practice of Solitude and Silence

1. De Waal, *The Celtic Way of Prayer*, 95.

2. David Adam, *Border Lands*, loc. 81, Kindle.

3. Seamus Heaney, *Preoccupations: Selected Prose 1968–1978* (London: Faber, 1980), 189.

4. John Philip Newell, *Christ of the Celts: The Healing of Creation* (San Francisco: Jossey-Bass, 2008), 24.

5. Mary Tardiff, O.P., ed., *At Home in the World: The Letters of Thomas Merton and Rosemary Radford Reuther* (Maryknoll, NY: Orbis, 1995), 35–36.

6. Sheldrake, *Living between Worlds*, 22.

10. The Practice of Seasonal Cycles

1. O'Donohue, *Anam Ċara*, xix.

2. De Waal, *The Celtic Way of Prayer*, 61–62.

3. Paintner, "St. Dearbhla's Eyes," originally published in *The Stinging Fly*, 13, no. 2 (Summer 2018): 89.

11. The Practice of Landscape as Theophany

1. O'Donohue, *Anam Ċara*, 37.

2. O'Donohue, *Anam Ċara*, 93.

3. Davies and O'Loughlin, *Celtic Spirituality*, 13.

4. Davies and O'Loughlin, *Celtic Spirituality*, 58.

5. Earle, *Celtic Christian Spirituality*, loc. 709–712.

12. The Practice of Three Essential Things

1. See p. 37 in Peter O'Dwyer's *Towards a History of Irish Spirituality*.

2. Georges Cerbelaud Salagnac and Bernadette Cerbelaud Salagnac, *Ireland: Isle of Saints* (Dublin: Clonmore and Reynolds, 1966), 80.

3. Ward, *Sayings of the Desert Fathers*, 37.

4. Ward, *Sayings of the Desert Fathers*, 44.

5. De Waal, *The Celtic Way of Prayer*, 40.

6. Jones, *Soul Making*, 60.

7. Edward C. Sellner, *Wisdom of the Celtic Saints* (Notre Dame, IN: Ave Maria Press, 1993), 142.

8. Paintner, originally published in *Spiritus: A Journal of Christian Spirituality* 17, no. 1 (Spring 2017): 111.

Appendix 1

1. This appendix has been excerpted from Christine Valters Paintner, *Lectio Divina—The Sacred Art: Transforming Words and Images into Heart-Centered Prayer* (Woodstock, VT: SkyLight Paths Publishing, 2011), 12–13.

Christine Valters Paintner is the online abbess for Abbey of the Arts, a virtual monastery offering classes and resources on contemplative practice and creative expression. She earned a doctorate in Christian spirituality from the Graduate Theological Union in Berkeley, California, and achieved professional status as a registered expressive arts consultant and educator from the International Expressive Arts Therapy Association.

Paintner is the author of eleven books on monasticism and creativity, including *The Wisdom of the Body*; *The Eyes of the Heart*; *Water, Wind, Earth, and Fire*; *The Artist's Rule*; *The Soul of a Pilgrim*; and *Illuminating the Way*. She leads pilgrimages in Ireland, Austria, and Germany and online retreats at her website, *AbbeyoftheArts.com*, living out her commitment as a Benedictine Oblate in Galway, Ireland, with her husband, John.

abbeyofthearts.com
Twitter: @abbeyofthearts
Facebook: @AbbeyoftheArts

MORE BOOKS BY
Christine Valters Paintner

The Soul of a Pilgrim
Eight Practices
for the Journey Within

The Artist's Rule
Nurturing Your Creative Soul
with Monastic Wisdom

Illuminating the Way
Embracing the Wisdom
of Monks and Mystics

Eyes of the Heart
Photography as a Christian
Contemplative Practice

The Wisdom of the Body
A Contemplative Journey
to Wholeness for Women

Water, Wind, Earth, and Fire
The Christian Practice
of Praying with the Elements